Projects for Woodworkers

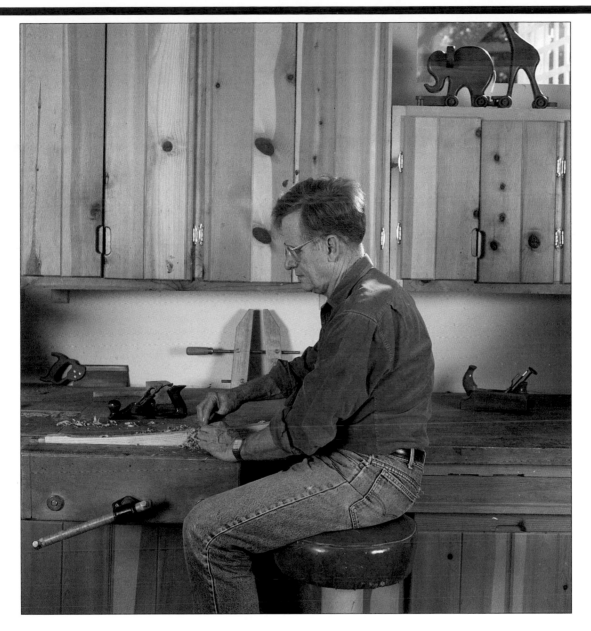

Created and Designed by the Editorial Staff of Ortho Books

Editors
Robert J. Beckstrom
Sally W. Smith

Writer
John Birchard

Photographers
Kenneth Rice
Jess Shirley

Illustrators
Angela Hildebrand
Ron Hildebrand

Ortho Books

Publisher
Robert Loperena

Editorial Director
Christine Jordan

Manufacturing Director
Ernie S. Tasaki

Managing Editor
Sally W. Smith

Editor
Robert J. Beckstrom

Prepress Supervisor
Linda M. Bouchard

Editorial Assistants
Joni Christiansen
Sally J. French

No portion of this book may be reproduced without written permission from the publisher.

We are not responsible for unsolicited manuscripts, photographs, or illustrations.

Every effort has been made at the time of publication to guarantee the accuracy of the names and addresses of information sources and suppliers, and in the technical data and recommendations contained. However, readers should check for their own assurance and must be responsible for selection and use of suppliers, supplies, materials, and chemical products.

Address all inquiries to:
Ortho Books
Box 5006
San Ramon, CA 94583-0906

Copyright © 1995
Monsanto Company
All rights reserved under international and Pan-American copyright conventions.

1 2 3 4 5 6 7 8 9
95 96 97 98 99 2000

ISBN 0-89721-258-4
Library of Congress Catalog Card
Number 94-69603

THE SOLARIS GROUP
2527 Camino Ramon
San Ramon, CA 94583-0906

Editorial Coordinator
Cass Dempsey

Copyeditor
Barbara Feller-Roth

Consultant
Sandor Nagyszalanczy

Special Thanks to
Deborah Cowder
Fred Sotcher

Proofreader
David Sweet

Indexer
Elinor Lindheimer

Separations by
Color Tech Corp.

Lithographed in the USA by
Banta Company

Front Cover

From simple to complex, practical to whimsical, this sampling represents the wide range of projects featured in this book. They include:

Left column, top to bottom: Victorian Gate, page 74; Hall Clock, page 35; Trestle Kitchen Table, page 32.

Center column, top to bottom: Child's Rocking Chair, page 22; Traditional Toolbox, page 6; Fisherman Whirligig, page 79; Storage Chest, page 13.

Right column, top to bottom: a Chest of Drawers, page 44; a Plywood Tulip Chair, page 26; an Early American Armoire, page 50.

Title Page

Each piece of a wood project is a miniproject of its own. Here, a scraper smooths and shapes the handle for a toolbox like the one shown on page 6; the curve was cut first on a band saw. Note the tenon at the end of the board.

Page 3

Top: This Plate Display Cabinet, presented on page 42, features dado joints, simple drawer construction, and decorative moldings that you can make yourself or buy from a lumberyard.

Bottom: Your stereo equipment, CDs, tapes, television, VCR, and other electronic gear will fit nicely into this entertainment-center armoire with elements of Gothic style (see page 55).

Back Cover

Top left: An electric router, with a ½-inch-diameter straight bit, cuts a groove into a piece of ¾-inch-thick stock. The depth adjustment on the router can be set for the desired depth of the groove, and a straightedge clamped to the board guides the tool in a straight line.

Top right: Ripping a board to exact width is easy work with a table saw. With the movable fence (shown behind the yellow push block) clamped into position, the operator has a steady guide for the board as he pushes it toward the blade.

Bottom left: Precision drilling, with the holes perfectly centered and drilled at a precise 90-degree angle, can be done on a drill press or with an electric drill guided by a doweling jig, as shown here.

Bottom right: The traditional way of making dovetail joints is with a backsaw, shown here, or a dovetail saw. These saws have fine teeth and stiff, reinforced blades to ensure clean, straight cuts.

Before purchasing any materials, cutting them, or proceeding with building a project, be sure that you have read and studied all of the instructions and that you understand each step of the process. Every effort has been made to ensure accuracy in the design, drawings, and descriptions of all projects, but the reader must accept final responsibility for any project built from these plans.

When using tools, equipment, or other products, observe all safety precautions of the manufacturer in the use of these tools or products, especially power tools, adhesives, and finishes.

Please note that the illustrations are renderings, not scale drawings. Measurements should not be taken directly from them. Instead, use dimensions specified in the materials lists, text, or—where included—the illustrations.

Projects for Woodworkers

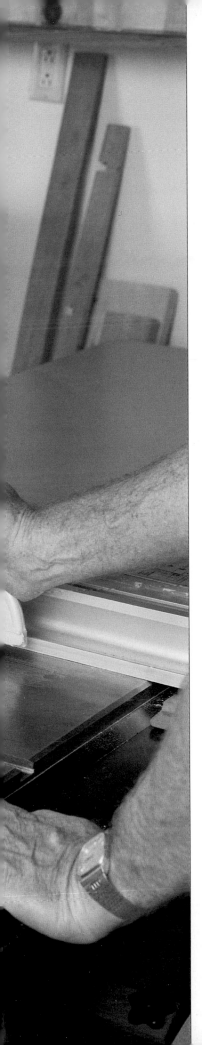

SIMPLE PROJECTS

The 25 projects in this book range in difficulty from simple boxes to complex storage pieces. Some can be built by anyone with basic woodworking skills and a few simple tools. Others will be a rewarding challenge for most hobbyists, requiring a modest woodworking shop and several weekends or evenings to complete.

The first chapter presents seven projects for getting started. Most of them are variations on a box, each with a detail or two for expanding the beginner's repertoire of basic skills and giving the piece some flair.

The next chapter presents projects for furnishing or decorating your home, followed by a chapter with more complex storage pieces. The fourth chapter features projects for the shop and yard.

Starting on page 82 is a quick refresher on woodworking techniques. Refer to it, as well as other projects, to learn any techniques or terminology that you aren't sure of.

Before operating any shop tool, be sure that it is equipped with safety guards and that you are familiar with safe operating techniques. This table saw has a blade guard and a splitter, a vertical fin behind the blade to keep the two halves of the board separated so they won't bind the blade. The out-feed table behind the saw and a push block also ensure safe operation, as do safety glasses and ear protection for the operator.

RADITIONAL TOOLBOX

Reflecting centuries of tradition, this toolbox is easy to carry, easy to load and unload, and very durable. The long compartments can hold saws and other large tools and even small power tools. The notches and holes in the crosspieces and the center divider will help organize smaller tools. No serious do-it-yourselfer should be without a box like this.

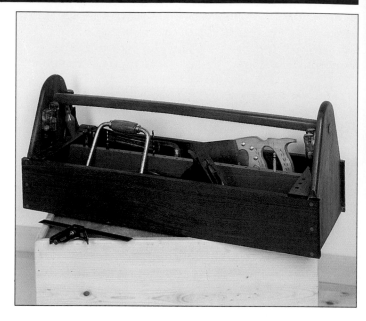

Tools required are a table saw or radial arm saw; a saber saw (jigsaw) or band saw; a drill with various bits including a pilot-hole cutter for #8 screws; a sharp ¾-inch chisel; and a router with a quarter-rounding bit (or a rasp or spokeshave).

This box is made from scraps of mahogany and other tropical hardwoods. If you prefer, use a tight-grain domestic hardwood such as maple or white oak. For the bottom, use ½-inch plywood or solid wood.

Detail of Handle

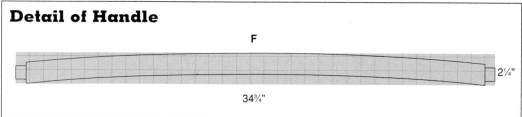

F

2¼"

34¾"

Exploded View

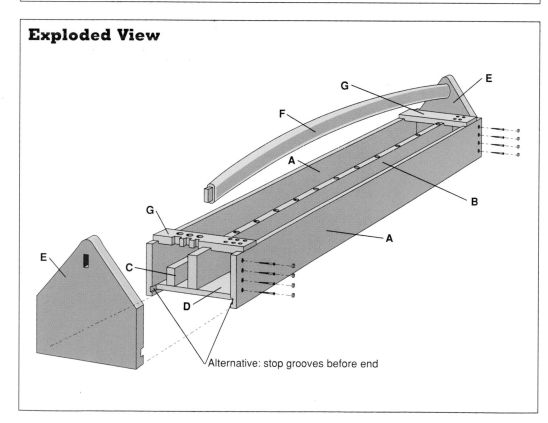

Alternative: stop grooves before end

1. Cutting the box parts

Begin by cutting the sides (A), the dividers (B and C), and the bottom (D). Be sure that these pieces are straight and free of knots. If necessary, plane any warps in the sides or partitions; leave the middle partition thick enough for the ½-inch-diameter holes.

Cut the ends (E) from wide, solid stock. They carry the entire weight of the box, so use only strong, tight-grain material that is free of warp and splits. Expand the pattern (see detail) and use it to lay out the through mortise for the handle tenon as well as the top and angle cuts. Use a plane or rasp, and eventually a sander, to smooth the cut edges.

Cut grooves in the sides and dadoes in the ends, ¼ inch from the bottoms, using a dado cutter or router bit that will cut a ½-inch-wide groove, set to a depth of ¼ inch. You can cut the dadoes all the way to the ends. However, with a router, you can start and stop ½ inch from each end, so that the dadoes won't show.

2. Making the handle

Make the handle from a 2¼-inch-wide piece of 2-by material that has been planed or resawed down to 1¼-inch thickness.

First cut the shoulders for the tenons with a table saw or radial arm saw. The tenons are ¾ inch long by ¾ inch wide by 1¼ inches high, so the shoulders will be ¼ inch wide. Because of the arc in the handle, the shoulder cuts will be ¾ inch from the top edge of the stock. Make parallel cuts from the shoulder to the end of each tenon, then use a sharp chisel to remove the rest of the waste. Now mark the arcs on the side 1¼ inches apart, and cut them with a saber saw or band saw. Round all four corners of the piece with a router with a ⅜- or ½-inch quarter-rounding bit set in a router table, or with a rasp, plane, spokeshave, or even coarse sandpaper. If you use the router, you'll still want to go back and finish shaping and sanding the piece to remove marks and irregularities.

Check the tenon size against the layout marks for the mortises on the end pieces to be sure that you don't make the mortises too large, then bore out the mortise holes with a ¾-inch bit and square the holes with a sharp chisel. So as not to chip out wood, bore the holes carefully and work from both faces to the middle with the chisel.

3. Assembling the box

Dry-assemble the box with the bottom and handle in place to be sure that everything fits. Then disassemble and apply glue to the meeting surfaces of the sides, the bottom, and the ends, and the mortises and tenons of the handle. Clamp the pieces together, being sure that the ends are seated tightly against the shoulders of the handle tenons. Thoroughly wipe away any excess glue with a damp rag. Use a pilot-hole cutter to bore the pilot holes and counterbores for the screws. Insert the screws, then plug the holes. Allow the glue to dry completely, then chisel and sand down the plugs.

Bore ½-inch-diameter holes in the top edge of the middle divider, then mark its position on the bottom inside of the box. Bore several screw holes down through the bottom of the box between the lines just marked, then clamp or hold the divider in place; bore up from below through the holes to make pilot holes in the divider. Secure the divider with 1¼-inch by #8 screws. Use the same method for the short divider.

Cut the crosspieces (G) for holding tools. They are rabbeted on the ends and dadoed in the middle to fit over the sides and middle divider. These cuts can be made with the table saw or radial arm saw, or by setting up a dado cutter. Attach the crosspieces to the box with glue and 4d finishing nails. Sand with an orbital sander with 100-grit sandpaper; finish with oil and wax.

Detail of End

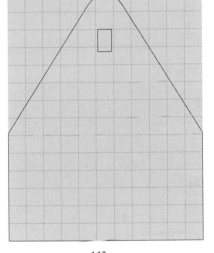

14"

11"

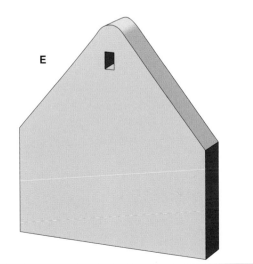

E

Materials List

Dimensions are finished size (inches), except for handle stock.

Part	Qty.	Description	Size/Material
A	2	Sides	¾ × 6 × 35 hardwood
B	1	Middle divider	¾ × 6 × 32⅛ hardwood
C	1	Short divider	¾ × 3½ × 32⅛ hardwood
D	1	Bottom	½ × 11⅜ × 33¾ plywood
E	2	Ends	¾ × 11 × 14 hardwood
F	1	Handle stock	1¼ × 2¼ × 34¾ hardwood
G	2	Crosspieces	¾ × 2½ × 12½ hardwood

Hardware

1¼" × #8 flat-head wood screws
4d finishing nails

SMALL BOOKCASE

This simple country-style bookcase, which will add a touch of warmth and beauty to any home, can be built in a day. To simplify it even more, you can make a back of ¼-inch plywood instead of installing the three separate back pieces. By lengthening the sides and adding more shelves, you can make the bookcase as tall as you like.

Tools required are a table saw or radial arm saw; a saber saw or band saw; a drill with a pilot-hole cutter; and several 36-inch-long bar clamps. You can use a dado blade to cut the dadoes for the shelves, but it's easier to use a router with a ¾-inch straight cutting bit, which is also less likely to tear out the grain around the cut.

Pine, cherry, or oak give the most traditional look for a country piece such as this. Knotty pine (#2 or #3 pine) 1 × 12 boards will work just fine as long as they are not warped or cracked; a hardwood will produce a more elegant finished piece.

1. Cutting the side pieces

Cut the 2 side pieces (A) to length and width; do not cut the curves yet. Lay the pieces out edge to edge on a workbench with their inside surfaces up; use a square to mark across them for the ¾-inch-wide dadoes that will hold the shelves. The tops of the shelves are 3¾ inches, 17½ inches, and 28½ inches from the bottom edge of the side pieces. Cut the dadoes ¼ inch deep.

2. Shaping the side pieces

Mark a line 1 inch in from the front edge of each side piece, starting at the top and ending 11½ inches from the top edge. Use a compass or a circular object to trace the curves at the top front corner of the side and just above the middle shelf. The curve above the middle shelf should start where the line ends and intersect the front edge of the side piece 13 inches below the top. Now use a saber saw to cut the upper part of the side pieces along these lines.

Expand the pattern for the decorative cuts on the bottom edges of the side pieces and transfer it to the side pieces. Cut along the pattern lines with the saber saw.

Exploded View

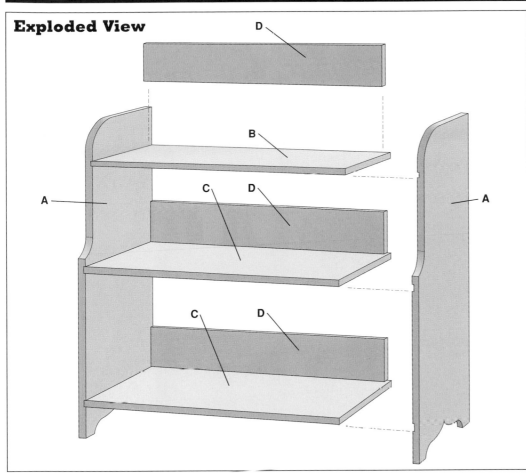

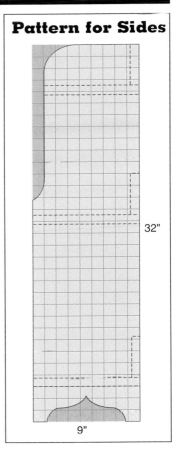

32"

9"

Materials List

Dimensions are finished size (in inches). Dimensions for curved piece are for stock from which piece is cut.

Part	Qty.	Description	Size/Material
A	2	Sides	¾ × 9 × 32 hardwood
B	1	Top shelf	¾ × 8 × 29 hardwood
C	2	Lower shelves	¾ × 9 × 29 hardwood
D	3	Back pieces	½ × 3½ × 28½ hardwood

Hardware

2" drywall screws
8d finishing nails

3. Cutting the shelves

The shelves (B and C) can be crosscut with a circular saw or handsaw. Be sure they're all the same length, and squarely cut in both directions. Note that the top shelf (B) is 1 inch narrower than the bottom shelves.

4. Joining the shelves to the sides

Apply glue to the dadoes for the shelves and to the ends of the shelves. Clamp the assembly together with bar clamps (see page 88). Finishing nails (8d) can be driven through the sides and into the shelves to strengthen the joints, but the nails aren't really necessary if you have enough clamps (at least 6) to make strong glue joints. Thoroughly wipe away all excess glue with a damp rag, and check to be sure that the assembly is square while it dries.

5. Attaching the back pieces

Cut the 3 back pieces (D) carefully so that they fit snugly between the side pieces without forcing them apart. Cut them from straight stock so that they don't cause the shelves to take on a warp. Apply a thin bead of glue to the bottom edges and ends of the back pieces, and clamp them in place on the shelves so that their back surfaces are flush with the back edges of the shelves and sides. Thoroughly wipe away any excess glue with a damp rag. Use a pilot-hole cutter to bore one or two pilot holes for screws in the bottoms of the shelves, and drive 2-inch drywall screws up from below into the back pieces. Finishing nails (8d) can also be driven through the side pieces and into the ends of the back pieces.

Set the nails and fill the depressions with wood putty. Sand the entire piece with fine sandpaper; finish with several thin coats of varnish or oil.

COUNTRY SPICE RACK

Here's a simple project that will add charm to any kitchen. This rack can be hung on a wall or the end of a cabinet, or on the inside of a pantry or cabinet door. It affords easy access to and easy viewing of all the savory additives in your culinary collection.

Tools required are a table saw or radial arm saw; a band saw; either a coping saw or saber saw (jigsaw); a router with a ½-inch straight cutting bit; and a drill with a ½-inch bit. A few short bar clamps will be helpful.

This spice rack is made from black walnut, but virtually any solid wood will work fine. The shelves could be made from ½-inch plywood, since no edges are exposed.

1. Cutting the sides

Cut the 2 side pieces (A). Use a round object (a spice jar would be about right) to mark the curve on the top outside corners. Cut the curves with a band saw or saber saw, then smooth the edges that will show with a hand plane and sanders.

2. Cutting the dadoes

Lay the side pieces edge to edge on a worktable with their inside surfaces up. Measure up from the bottom edge 1 inch, and use a square to draw a line across both pieces at right angles to the front and back edges. This will be the bottom of the lowest shelf. At 5½-inch intervals up from this line, draw 5 more lines across the

sides at right angles to the front and back edges. These lines indicate the bottom edges of the remaining shelves. Use a router with a ½-inch straight cutting bit and a clamp-on straightedge to cut the dadoes that will hold the shelves. Each dado should be ¼ inch deep.

3. Cutting and gluing the shelves

Plane or resaw (on a table saw) a 6-foot length of 3-inch-wide stock down to ½-inch thickness for the shelves (B) (or use a scrap of ½-inch plywood). Cut the shelves, sand them if necessary, and check to be sure that they will all fit in the dadoes in the side pieces. Brush glue into all the slots and onto the ends of the shelves, and use short bar clamps (see page 88) to bring the sides in tight on the shelves and hold them until the glue dries. Thoroughly wipe away all excess glue with a damp rag. Before setting the assembly aside to dry, measure both diagonals to be sure that the assembly is square.

Materials List

Dimensions are finished size (in inches). Dimensions for curved pieces are for stock from which piece is cut.

Part	Qty.	Description	Size/Material
A	2	Side pieces	¾ × 3 × 34 hardwood
B	6	Shelves	½ × 3 × 11 hardwood or plywood
C	6	Front pieces	³⁄₁₆ × 2 × 12 hardwood
Hardware			

1" × #16 brass brads, or escutcheon pins
Brass-plated L brackets

4. Cutting the front pieces

Expand the pattern for the front pieces (C), and transfer it to 2 pieces of ¾-inch-thick solid stock. Cut the curved pattern on the upper edge of the pieces with the band saw or saber saw. Cut the hearts

freehand with the saber saw, or follow this method: Create the upper curves by drilling 2 overlapping holes with a ½-inch bit. To mark the centers of the curves, use a square to draw a line at right angles to the bottom edge at the midpoint of the board. Draw

Exploded View

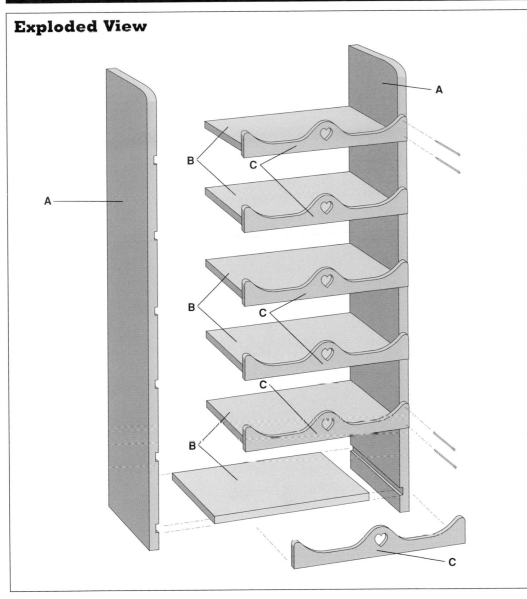

Pattern for Front Pieces

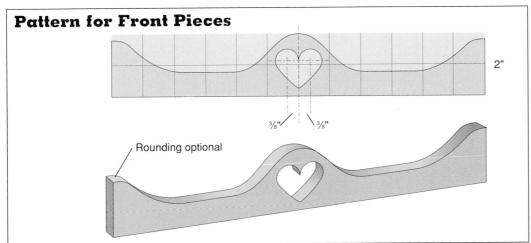

2"

⅜" ⅜"

Rounding optional

another line ⅜ inch away from the centerline on each side. Now mark a horizontal line through all 3 lines 1¼ inches from the bottom edge. Center the drill bit on the intersection of the horizontal line and one outer vertical line, and drill through the piece; repeat at the other intersection. Use a coping saw or saber saw to cut out the rest of the heart shape, being careful to keep the lower tip of the cutout at least ½ inch above the bottom edge of the piece. When you have done this on both pieces, use either the band saw or table saw to cut each ¾-inch-thick piece into 3 pieces, each about ³⁄₁₆ inch thick if you use the band saw, less if you use the table saw with a ⅛-inch-thick blade. If you use the table saw, be careful to use a push stick for this very thin stock. Sand the pieces to remove sawing marks, and to slightly round and smooth the edges.

5. Attaching the front pieces

Lay the front pieces in place with their bottom edges flush with the bottom edges of the shelves. Use a ¹⁄₁₆-inch bit to predrill the holes for the brads that will hold the front pieces in place. Tack the pieces in place with 4 to 6 brass brads (1 inch by #16), called escutcheon pins, in each piece.

Finish the rack with oil or varnish. Small brass-plated L brackets can be used either below or above the shelves to mount the rack.

BOXES—THREE VARIATIONS

To change the sizes of these easy-to-build boxes, you can enlarge the dimensions, or reduce them and use ¼- or ½-inch plywood. The miter corners and banded edges conceal the rough edges of plywood, but you can substitute solid lumber. Paint, stain, or seal the boxes, or decorate them with painted or stenciled designs—the choices are almost endless.

Tools required are an accurate tilting arbor table saw with a fine-toothed blade; a band saw or saber saw (jigsaw); and a router with a ⅜-inch quarter-rounding bit. Band or miter clamps and a few small bar clamps will be helpful.

Variation #1— Storage Chest With Stand

This chest is just the right size for storing record albums, but it could also work as a small file cabinet. A flatter version, possibly with a tray or shelf inside, would make an attractive jewelry box. This chest is made with ½-inch birch plywood (solid birch for the stand); it

is stained on the inside and painted on the outside.

1. Cutting the sides

Begin by cutting the front and back (A) and the end pieces (B), with all 4 edges of each piece cut square. Then set a table saw blade to a 45° angle for making the miter cuts where the front, back, and ends meet. Check your cut on a couple of pieces of scrap to be sure that it is accurate.

2. Cutting the top and bottom

Check the results of your miter cutting by using 2 band clamps to clamp all 4 pieces together (no glue). If necessary, you can plane or recut to

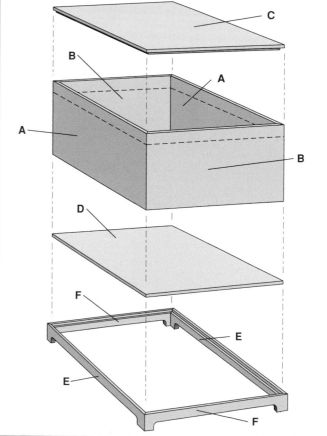

Materials List, Variation #1

Dimensions are finished size (in inches). Dimensions for curved pieces are for stock from which piece is cut.

Part	Qty.	Description	Size/Material
A	2	Front and back	½ × 14 × 23 plywood
B	2	Ends	½ × 14 × 14 plywood
C	1	Top	½ × 14 × 23 plywood
D	1	Bottom	¼ × 14 × 23 plywood
E	2	Stand sides	¾ × 3 × 23¾ birch
F	2	Stand ends	¾ × 3 × 14¾ birch

Hardware

2 brass butt hinges (2" × 1")
8" brass chain
1½" brads or 5d finishing nails

Storage Chest With Stand, Exploded View

make the joints tight. Before unclamping the pieces, measure from outside to outside surface to verify the length and width for the top and bottom (C and D), then cut these pieces out square on the table saw. With the table saw or router, cut a rabbet all the way around the top so that it will fit down into the front, back, and ends. This rabbet should be ½ inch wide and ⅜ inch deep. This leaves only ⅛ inch of the plywood edge showing around the top; when this is rounded slightly by sanding, it becomes nearly unnoticeable.

3. Assembling the chest

Spread glue evenly on all the miter cuts, then clamp the front, back, and ends back together. Drive several 1½-inch brads or 5d finishing nails through each miter joint from both directions to reinforce the joints. Avoid nails 2 inches from the top, where you will be sawing into the chest. With a damp rag, thoroughly wipe away any excess glue, especially on the inside. Then put the top in place to check its fit. It should fit snugly without pushing the corner joints apart. Plane or recut the rabbet if the corners are separating, then apply glue around the rabbet, and nail the top to the chest with small nails every 6 inches. Spread glue sparingly on the bottom edges of the chest and nail the bottom in place. To cut the chest lid, set the fence on the table saw about 2 inches from the blade, and cut all the way around the chest (see dashed line in the drawing).

4. Milling the stand pieces

Rip the stand pieces (E and F) to a width of 3 inches, and rough-cut them a couple of inches long to start. Next cut a rabbet along the inside top edges of all 4 pieces, ¼ inch wide and ⅜ inch deep (when viewed from the back), so that the bottom of the chest will nest completely in the stand. Now make the miter cuts at the ends of the stand pieces. Make the cut on one end (using a miter saw or table saw), then hold the piece against the bottom of the chest with the cut lined up at one corner, and mark the point where the other corner of the chest intersects the back of the stand piece. Cut the second miter through this mark. Cut all 4 pieces this way; use the band clamps to hold them together while you check to see if the chest fits into the rabbet; adjust if necessary.

Now make the curved cuts on the bottoms of the stand pieces. Scribe a horizontal line along each piece 1½ inches from the bottom, and a vertical line 1½ inches from each end. Using a compass or tin can, draw a curve with a 1½-inch radius where the lines intersect. Cut these lines with a band saw or saber saw, then use a ⅜-inch quarter-rounding bit in the router that is mounted in a router table to round the outer edges of both the top and the bottom of each stand piece. After routing, use a drum sander, or a rasp and hand sanding, to smooth the curves along the bottom edges where necessary.

5. Attaching the stand to the chest

Dry-fit the base pieces again to be sure that the chest fits snugly into the rabbets (shave the miters if it's loose). Apply glue to the miter cuts and use the band clamps to clamp the pieces together (see page 88). Drive small nails through the joints to reinforce them. After the glue has dried, apply a small amount of glue to the rabbet and use short bar clamps to hold the stand tightly to the chest until the glue has dried.

6. Finishing details

Conceal the exposed plywood edges on the top of the chest and the bottom of the lid by edge-banding them with veneer tape (see page 59). Screw 2- by 1-inch brass butt hinges to the back edges of the chest and lid, and 8 inches of brass chain to one end of

the chest and lid to keep the lid from flopping backward when it is open. Putty all nail holes, then sand the chest thoroughly, rounding all the sharp edges slightly. Paint, stain, or seal the chest to your preference.

Variation #2— Storage Chest With Beveled Base

This larger chest, which should be made from ¾-inch plywood, works well as either a blanket chest or a toy chest. However, if it is used as a toy chest, be sure to use lid supports, because falling lids can injure small children. This chest is made of cherry-veneered plywood, with solid cherry moldings and base pieces. Any type of plywood and matching solid wood could be used.

Storage Chest With Beveled Base, Exploded View

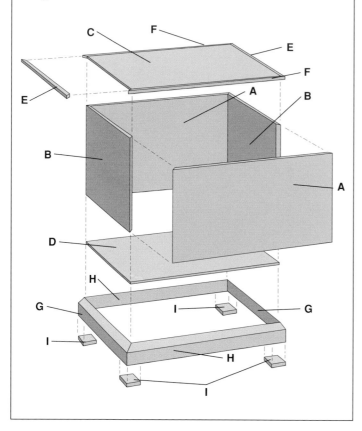

Materials List, Variation #2

Dimensions are finished size (in inches). Dimensions for curved pieces are for stock from which piece is cut.

Part	Qty.	Description	Size/Material
A	2	Front and back	¾ × 16 × 30 plywood
B	2	Ends	¾ × 16 × 16 plywood
C	1	Top	¾ × 16½ × 30½ plywood
D	1	Bottom	¼ × 16 × 30 plywood
E	2	Short moldings	¾ × ¾ × 18 half round
F	2	Long moldings	¾ × ¾ × 32 half round
G	2	Short base pieces	¾ × 3 × 18 hardwood
H	2	Long base pieces	¾ × 3 × 32 hardwood
I	4	Feet	¼ × 2 × 2 plywood

Hardware

1½" brads or 5d finishing nails
2 brass butt hinges (2" × 1")
Lid supports

1. Building the chest

Cut the front and back (A) and ends (B) of this chest and join them in the same manner as those for Variation #1. Cut the bottom (D) and glue and nail it to the front, back, and ends as for the first chest. Cut the top (C) and apply the half-round moldings (E and F) to its edges as shown, using glue and small brads and mitering the corners of the moldings.

2. Attaching the base

Rip the base pieces (G and H) to width. For now, cut them a little longer than needed. Bevel the top edge to a 45° angle. Sand or plane the surface of the 45° cut before proceeding. Now miter the pieces (do not rabbet them as in Variation #1), so that they fit around the bottom of the chest, overhanging it by ¼ inch. Use band clamps to clamp the pieces in place to check their fit, then apply glue to the miter cuts and the inside surfaces of the base pieces and clamp them in place. Drive small nails through the miter joints. Thoroughly wipe away any excess glue with a damp rag.

Cut the 4 foot pieces (I). Apply glue to the top surface of each foot, and position each foot under a corner of the base. Set the chest on a flat surface and allow the glue to dry.

3. Finishing the chest

Use veneer tape to cover the exposed plywood edges around the top (see page 59), and install the hinges. Follow manufacturer's instructions for the lid supports to mount them on one or both sides. Set and putty all nails, then sand and finish the chest.

Variation #3—Portable Bookshelf Boxes

These boxes are built in the same manner as the previous ones, except that the miter joints at the corners are reinforced with metal angle brackets (an optional hidden spline is also shown), and the bottoms are held in a groove to make them stronger. Designed to work as open bookshelves or as moving and storage boxes, they can be built of solid wood or plywood. Directions are for the largest box; vary them to make boxes of other sizes. If you use lumber, be sure to select straight, flat boards that are free of knots. If you use plywood, moldings or edge banding can be applied to the edges.

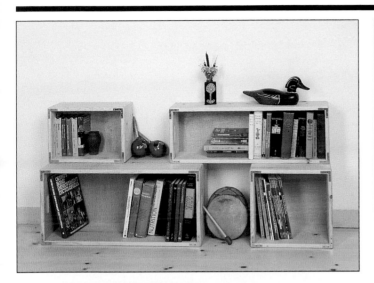

Materials List, Variation #3

Dimensions are finished size (in inches) for the longest box. Dimensions for curved pieces are for stock from which piece is cut.

Part	Qty.	Description	Size/Material
A	2	Front and back	¾ × 11½ × 30 pine
B	2	Ends	¾ × 11½ × 12 pine
C	1	Bottom	¼ × 11 × 29 plywood
D	4	Splines (opt.)	¼ × 1 × 11 hardwood
E	4	Short moldings (opt.)	¾ × ¾ × 12 half round
F	4	Long moldings (opt.)	¾ × ¾ × 30 half round

Hardware

4 angle brackets 3" × 3"
1½" finishing nails
1" × #8 flat-head wood screws

Portable Bookshelf Boxes, Exploded View

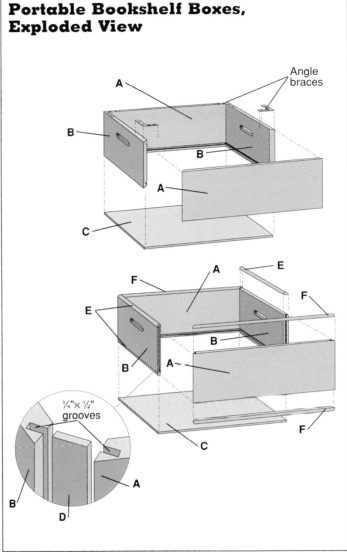

1. Cutting the pieces

The front and back (A) and ends (B) are made in the same manner as for Variation #1. However, before assembly, cut 1-inch by 3½-inch rounded hand holes in the ends with a fine-toothed saber-saw blade, then use a router with a ⅜-inch quarter-rounding bit to round both sides of the hand holes.

Also before assembly, cut a ¼-inch-wide by ¼-inch-deep groove, ¼ inch above the bottom edge of the sides and ends to hold the bottom (C). Cut out the bottom.

2. Assembling the box

Assemble the box as in Variation #1, except with the bottom in place in the grooves. When the glue has dried, apply the metal angle brackets with 1-inch by #8 screws.

Optional joinery: If you do not like the look of the metal angle brackets used to strengthen the corners of these boxes, a spline can be inserted in each miter joint instead. After the miters have been cut on all the side and end pieces, use either the table saw with a dado cutter, or a router with a ¼-inch straight cutting bit, to cut a ¼-inch-wide by ½-inch-deep groove through the face of each miter cut. The pieces must be held at a 45° angle so that the miter edge

stays firmly against the table-saw bed. To do this safely, build a pie-shaped box with a 45° sloped top on which to rest the pieces as you slide them across the saw bed. Cut 4¼-inch by 1-inch splines from solid stock. Apply glue to the miter faces, insert one spine in each corner, and clamp the box together with band clamps. Nail half-round moldings (E and F) to the top edges to cover the splines or plywood edges (if plywood is used).

WINE RACK

This easy-to-build wine rack can be freestanding or built into a cabinet. To increase or decrease the height or width, change the front and back crosspiece measurements in increments of 3¼ inches and the height of the side panels in 3½-inch increments. If you plan to store larger bottles, such as champagne, adjust the measurements accordingly.

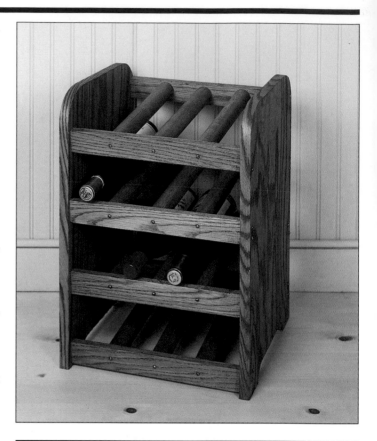

Tools required are a table saw or radial arm saw; a saber saw (jigsaw); a drill with a pilot-hole cutter; and a Phillips screwdriver. A couple of short bar clamps will be helpful.

Oak or cherry are beautiful and elegant woods to use for this piece, but it may be hard to find 11¼-inch-wide boards that are not warped. Pine or redwood could be substituted. The closet dowels are usually available only in Douglas fir, but this could be stained to match a darker wood.

1. Cutting the sides

The 2 side pieces (A) can be made from one piece of 1×12 that is slightly longer than 40 inches. Draw a line at right angles to the long edges through the middle of the board (see detail) and drill 2 holes, 1 inch in diameter, centered on this line and 3 inches in from either edge. Be sure to clamp a scrap board to the back while you drill the holes to avoid tear-out when the bit goes through. Draw a line on each side of the circles to connect them, as shown.

Cut through the centerline to separate the 2 side pieces, and use a jigsaw to cut along the lines between the 2 half holes to shape the bottom. Use a compass or a round object

to draw the quarter circles on the top corners of the 2 side pieces, and cut these corners round with the jigsaw as well.

If you wish to cut slots in the sides for handgrips, drill 1-inch-diameter holes 4¼ inches apart and 3½ inches from each side, and 2 inches from the end. Connect the holes and cut along the lines with a jigsaw.

2. Cutting the crosspieces

Cut 8 crosspieces (B) from 1×2 stock (you can rip your stock down from 1×12 if you prefer). The crosscuts on these pieces must be perfectly square, and the pieces must all be exactly the same length. This can be accomplished on either a table saw or radial arm saw by clamping a stop to the saw table (or crosscutting jig) to position each piece so that it will be exactly the same length as all the others.

3. Attaching the crosspieces

The bottom crosspieces go 1 inch above the bottom of the side pieces, and each additional crosspiece goes 3½ inches above the top of the one below it. Use bar clamps to hold the side pieces to the top and bottom crosspieces

while you drill pilot holes through the sides and into the ends of the crosspieces. Screw these 4 crosspieces in place and remove the clamps. Position the remaining 4 crosspieces, drill the pilot holes, and insert the screws in these as well. If you want to conceal the screwheads, counterbore the pilot holes.

Materials List

Dimensions are finished size (in inches). Dimensions for curved pieces are for stock from which piece is cut.

Part	Qty.	Description	Size/Material
A	2	Side pieces	¾ × 11¼ × 20 hardwood
B	8	Crosspieces	¾ × 1½ × 12¾ hardwood
C	12	Dowels	9¾ × 1¼ closet dowel
Hardware			

56 brass or panhead screws (2" × #8)
56 screw plugs (⅜", optional)

4. Installing the dowels

Use the same kind of crosscutting stop that you used in step 2 to cut the sections of 1¼-inch closet dowel for the bottle supports (C). Be sure that these cuts are perfectly square. Position the supports as shown, drill pilot holes, and insert screws to hold them in place. To conceal the screwheads, counterbore the pilot holes.

Exploded View

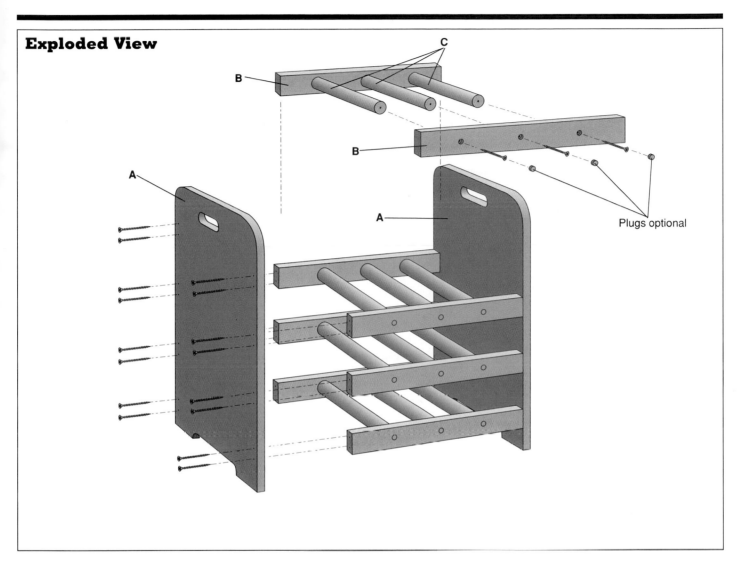

C

B

B

A

A

Plugs optional

Pattern for Sides

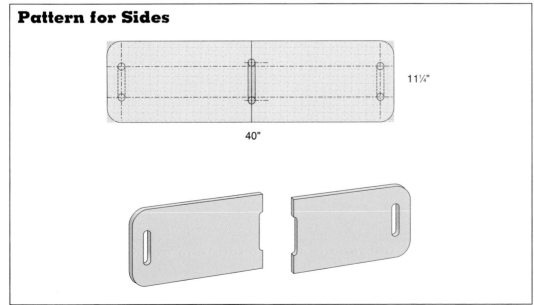

11¼"

40"

5. Completing the rack

If you are concealing the screwheads, use a plug cutter to make plugs, or buy precut, tapered plugs. Squeeze a drop of glue into each counterbored screw hole and tap a plug into place. When the glue has dried, use a sharp chisel or coarse sandpaper on a belt or disk sander to cut the plugs down flush to the surrounding wood. Sand the entire piece with 100-grit sandpaper, rounding the edges slightly and removing saw marks and other work marks. Finish with stain, oil, or varnish.

FURNITURE PROJECTS

Each of the seven projects in this chapter requires one or two operations beyond basic cutting and simple joinery techniques. Most projects include dowel joints, which are easy to do if you have a doweling jig for the accurate drilling of holes. One project, the Trestle Kitchen Table (see page 32), includes mortise-and-tenon joints and tapered cuts. Some projects, though simple in design, require handling large pieces of lumber or plywood. Some projects include simple jigs that you can build for performing specific tasks, such as drilling dowels in wide stock (Hall Clock, see page 35). The two table projects and the Country Bench (see page 20) have wide slabs made from joining two or more pieces of lumber together lengthwise, which may require a jointer or planer to straighten the meeting edges of the boards before you edge-join them. If you have a router, or need an excuse to buy one, many of these projects have edge shapes, grooves, dadoes, or other details that are done most easily with this indispensable workshop tool.

The basic tools for making a dowel joint are a drill and a doweling jig. This jig, one of several styles available, has been clamped onto the edge of a board so the hole corresponding to the drill bit size is centered over a mark that aligns with one of the holes already drilled into the mating board.

COUNTRY BENCH

This easy-to-build bench is based on the design of an old country church pew and is meant to be used anywhere indoors, such as at the foot of a bed, in a child's room, or in a breakfast nook.

Tools required are a drill with a doweling jig and a ⅜-inch bit; a band saw or saber saw (jigsaw); a router with a ¾-inch straight cutting bit; and a portable circular saw or table saw. A Phillips screwdriver, pilot-hole cutter for the drill, and some short bar clamps will also be helpful.

Pine or oak will produce the most traditional look for this piece, but it could also be made with birch and birch plywood if you want to paint it.

1. Gluing the end stock

Join the stock for the 2 end pieces (A) from one piece each of 2 × 12 material and 2 × 8 material. Position the pieces edge to edge and check to be sure that they will fit together tightly; you may have to trim the edges with a table saw, or joint or plane them to get a good fit. Use a doweling jig to drill holes for the dowel pins near each end and in the middle of the adjoining edges of each piece, then apply glue along the meeting edges, on the dowel pins, and in the holes, insert the dowel pins, and use short bar clamps (see page 88) to bring the pieces together. Check with a straightedge to be sure that the assemblies are flat, then thoroughly wipe away any excess glue with a damp rag, and set the pieces aside.

2. Shaping the ends

Expand the pattern for the end pieces to full size. When the glue has dried, use a saber saw to carefully cut the pieces to shape. Clamp the 2 end pieces together and use a rasp, plane, grinder, sander, or whatever tools you have to smooth the cuts and remove all saw marks from the edges. You can also use a router with either a quarter-rounding bit or a chamfering bit to ease the edges all the way around. Be sure to round the corners of the feet, both front and back, so that they will not tend to splinter when being scooted around the floor.

3. Dadoing the ends

Lay the end pieces on a workbench with their back edges touching and their inside surfaces facing up. Measure up from the bottom front corner of each, and mark a point on the front edge 17 inches above the bottom. Now measure 5 inches in from the back and up from the bottom 16¼ inches and mark the intersection. Draw a line from the intersection to the mark on the front edge of each piece. This will be the bottom edge of the dado that will hold the seat. Use the router with a clamp-on straightedge and a ¾-inch straight cutting bit to cut a ½-inch-deep dado along each line, stopping at the mark that is 5 inches from the back of each

piece. Square up the dado end with a sharp chisel.

4. Cutting the seat and back pieces

Cut the seat (B) and the back (C), using a fine-toothed plywood cutting blade. Plane or joint if necessary to be sure that the front and back edges of the seat and the top edge of the back are perfectly square and straight. Also cut the 3 glue strips (D) that will go

below the seat and at the top of the back.

5. Assembling the bench

Use an ⅛-inch drill bit to drill through the center of the dado (from the inside) in 3 places on each end piece to position the screws that will help hold the ends to the seat. From the outside, use a pilot-hole cutter to cut a counterbore for each screw. Dry-fit the seat in the slots, checking to be sure that

Materials List

Dimensions are finished size (in inches). Dimensions for curved pieces are for stock from which piece is cut.

Part	Qty.	Description	Size/Material
A	2	End pieces	2 × 12 × 42 pine or oak
	2	End pieces	2 × 8 × 25 pine or oak
B	1	Seat	¾ × 14 × 48 veneered plywood
C	1	Back	¾ × 23 × 47 veneered plywood
D	3	Glue strips	¾ × ¾ × 47 pine or oak
E	1	Front edge piece	1½ × 2 × 48 pine or oak
F	1	Top edge molding	¾ × 1½ × 47 pine or oak

Hardware

2½" × #10 flat-head wood screws
1¼" drywall screws
⅜" dowel pins
5d finishing nails

it comes out flush with the front edges; then apply glue in the dadoes and to the ends of the seat and use bar clamps to hold the ends to the seat while you drive in 2½-inch by #10 screws. Slide the back into place so that it is square to the seat and extends down about 1 inch past its bottom edge. Scribe lines on the end pieces to show where the back will go, then remove the back and drill and counterbore the screw holes for it. Also, drill pilot holes along the bottom of the back for screwing it to the seat. Finally, apply glue to the ends of the back and to the back edge of the seat, and clamp the back in position while you insert the screws through both the ends and the back (into the seat). Squeeze a little glue in all the counter-bore holes and insert plugs to cover the screws. Thoroughly wipe away any excess glue with a damp rag. After the glue has partially dried, use a plane, rasp, or sander to cut the plugs down flush to the surfaces of the ends.

Pattern

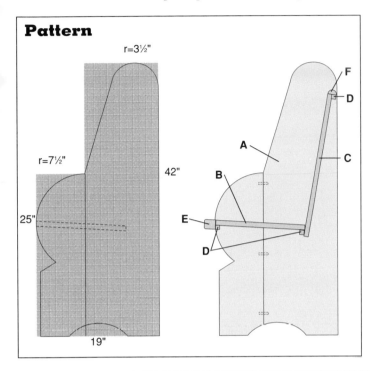

Exploded View

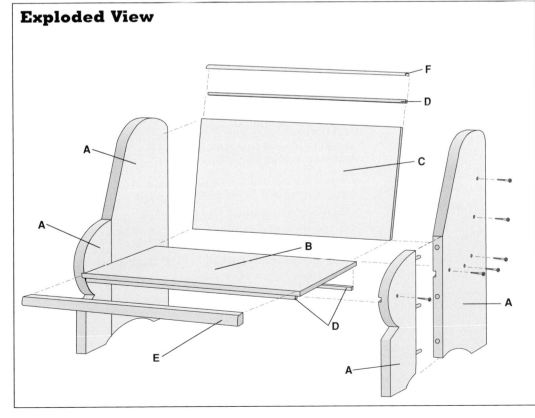

6. Attaching the edge pieces

Cut the front edge piece (E) and round the ends with the band saw or saber saw. Use the router with a quarter-rounding bit to round its top and bottom edges. Check the fit against the front edge of the seat. Then apply glue to the edge of the seat and use short bar clamps to clamp the edge piece in place. Its top surface should be flush with the top edge of the seat. Thoroughly wipe away any excess glue with a damp rag. Secure the edge piece with screws driven at an angle, through the plywood into the edge piece. Drill pilot holes first.

Apply the top edge molding (F) in the same manner as the front edge piece, but use 5d finishing nails to hold it in place (predrill). The front edge of the molding should be flush with the front surface of the back.

7. Attaching the glue strips

The 3 glue strips can now be glued and screwed or nailed in place to help reinforce the edge pieces and the joint between the seat and the back. To attach the strips to the seat and front edge piece, and the seat and back, use 1¼-inch drywall screws; drill pilot holes for the screws, then apply glue to 2 sides of each strip. The top molding is too thin for screws; use 5d finishing nails.

Set the nails along the top edge, putty the holes, and sand the entire piece with 120-grit sandpaper to remove all glue and other defects. Finish with varnish or oil.

CHILD'S ROCKING CHAIR

Rocking chairs have enduring appeal to people of all ages. This child-size one is simple to build and sturdy enough to last through several generations. Yours could easily become a family heirloom.

Tools required are a table saw or radial arm saw; a band saw or saber saw (jigsaw); a router with a large-diameter quarter-rounding bit and a ⅜-inch straight cutting bit; a drill with a countersink bit, a doweling jig, and a ⅜-inch bit; and bar clamps. A belt sander would be helpful for removing saw marks from the rockers, and an orbital sander for finish sanding.

Any hardwood will work well for this project, but if you choose a lighter-colored one such as oak or maple, you may want to stain or paint it. An oil or light varnish finish will protect and highlight the natural beauty of darker woods.

1. Cutting the frame pieces

Begin by cutting the 2 side rails (C), the four uprights (D), and the armrests (E). Cut ½-inch by ½-inch rabbets on either side of the top end of the 4 uprights (see detail, page 24) to form the tenons that fit into the mortises in the bottom of the armrests. These short tenons, called stub tenons, can be cut with either a handsaw or power saw. Sand each piece individually as you proceed, to remove saw marks. Be careful not to remove too much wood; the joint must be tight.

2. Assembling the side frames

Measure down 5½ inches from the top of each tenon and mark the spot on the upright where the top edge of the side rail will intersect it. Lay out the side rails and uprights in final position, and mark across the joints with a square for the dowel pins that will hold the pieces together. Use a doweling jig to drill ⅜-inch by 1-inch holes for the dowel pins in the side rails and uprights; apply glue to the ends of the side rails, the dowel pins, and in the holes, and insert the dowel pins. Use bar clamps (see page 88) to press the uprights to the side rails. Thoroughly wipe away any excess glue with a damp rag and set the assembly aside to dry.

3. Cutting the armrests

Use a saber saw, coping saw, or band saw to make the curved cuts at the back of the armrests (E), then place the armrests on the upright-and-side-rail assembly. Mark the position of the mortises on the undersides of the armrests.

The front mortise should start ¾ inch back from the front edge and should be ½ inch in from the inside edge. The back mortise should be ½ inch in from the inside edge and 3¼ inches from the back end of the armrest. Check your layout marks by setting

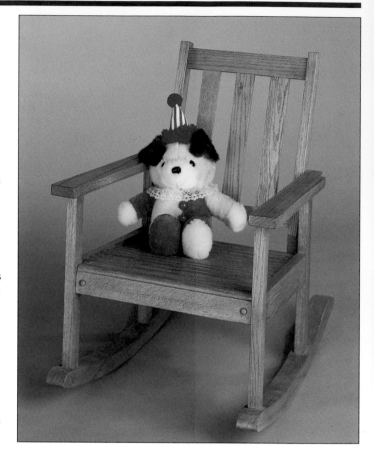

the armrests on the uprights to see if the marks align with the tenons. Make any necessary adjustments.

Use a ¼-inch drill bit with a depth stop set at ½ inch to bore out as much of the mortises as possible, then use a sharp chisel to complete them. Do not cut the mortises too large. It is better to cut them too tight at first, then gradually shave the corresponding leg tenons down until they fit snugly. Use a plane, chisel, or sandpaper to reduce the size of the tenon. If the joint is too loose, wrap the tenon with fine string to make a snug fit. Do not rely on glue to fill the gaps.

4. Gluing the armrests

After the glue holding the side rails to the uprights has dried overnight, test-fit the mortises and tenons. When the fit is satisfactory, apply glue to both the mortises and tenons and clamp the armrests onto the uprights. Check to be sure that the armrests are at right angles to the uprights. Thoroughly wipe away any excess glue with a damp rag, and set the frames aside to dry.

5. Cutting the rockers

Expand the pattern for the rockers (F) to full size and transfer it to 1½-inch-thick stock. The band saw will give the best results for cutting out the rockers, but you could also use a saber saw if you have a steady hand. Use a belt sander

Exploded View

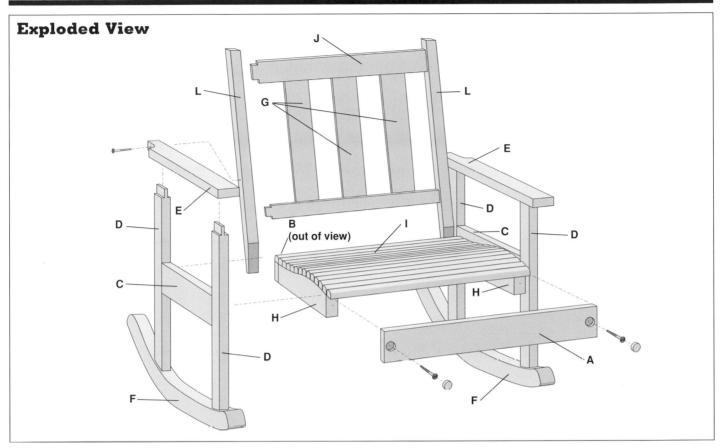

Materials List

Dimensions are finished size (in inches). Dimensions for shaped pieces are for stock from which piece is cut.

Part	Qty.	Description	Size/Material
A	1	Front rail	¾ × 1½ × 14 hardwood
B	1	Back rail	¾ × 1½ × 13 hardwood
C	2	Side rails	¾ × 2¼ × 10¾ hardwood
D	4	Uprights	¾ × 1 × 13 hardwood
E	2	Armrests	¾ × 2 × 15¾ hardwood
F	2	Rockers	(cut from 1½ × 3¼ × 22 hardwood)
G	3	Back slats	⅜ × 1½ × 11¼ hardwood
H	2	Seat support pieces	1½ × 2 × 11¼ hardwood
I	14	Seat slats	½ × ¾ × 14 (cut from ¾ × 6 × 28 stock)
J	1	Upper back rail	¾ × 2 × 11¾ hardwood
K	1	Lower back rail	¾ × 1¼ × 11¾ hardwood
L	2	Back uprights	¾ × 1 × 18

Hardware

1½" × #10 flat-head wood screws
2" × #10 flat-head wood screws
⅜" × 1" dowel pins (optional)

with a coarse belt to smooth and shape the curved edges.

6. Attaching the rockers

Hold the upright assemblies against the rockers so that the front upright is about 1½ inches behind the front end of the rocker, and mark the rocker curve on the bottoms of the uprights so that they can be trimmed to fit tightly down onto the rockers. Make these cuts with the saber saw or handsaw, and check the fit. Recut if necessary, or shave bits off with a chisel or plane until the fit is tight. Mark the top of the rocker where the uprights will land on it, then drill straight down through the center with an ⅛-inch bit

for the screws (one per upright) that will hold the rocker to the uprights. Turn the assembly upside down and position one rocker on the uprights. From the bottom of the rocker, use a countersink bit to cut the counterbores for the screws, and drill a pilot hole up into each upright. After applying glue to the rocker and uprights, drive the 2-inch by #10 screws to hold the rocker to the uprights. Repeat for the other rocker. (For a stronger joint, use ½-inch dowels, 2 inches long, instead of screws. Because a doweling jig would be too hard to align on the curved rockers, drill the ½-inch holes for the dowels from the bottom of the rockers into the uprights.)

Tenon Details

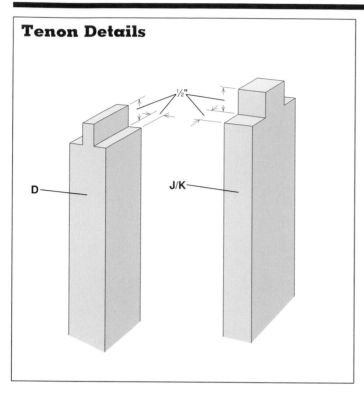

D   J/K   ½"

Top View of Seat

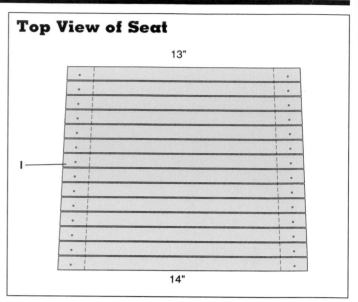

13"

I

14"

Rocker Pattern

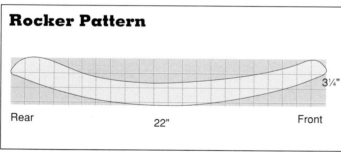

Rear   22"   Front   3¼"

7. Attaching the seat supports

Cut the seat support pieces (H) to length. With the band saw or saber saw, cut a gently curving contour into the top edge of each piece (see pattern on page 25). With the curved edges up, glue and screw the support pieces to the side rails so that they extend ¼ inch past each end of the side rails (this will leave exposed ¾ inch of upright, where the front or back rail will join it), and are flush with the bottom of the side rails.

8. Completing the seat frame

Cut the front and back rails (A and B) (notice that the back rail is 1 inch shorter than the front rail so that the chair will flair toward the front). The ends of these pieces should be beveled slightly so that the backs are a bit shorter than the fronts. They are close enough to square to cut them that way, then just sand or plane the ends slightly so that they fit tightly against the uprights. Apply glue to the ends of the seat support pieces; use

a pilot-hole cutter to predrill the holes for the 2-inch by #10 screws that hold the front and back rails in place. Insert a "button" plug in the pilot holes in the front rail only. The back screw holes will be covered by the back uprights. (If you expect the rocker to get vigorous use, join the front and back rails to the uprights with ⅜-inch dowel pins in addition to screwing them to the seat supports.)

9. Cutting the back pieces

Cut the pieces for the back. The back slats (G) are only ⅜ inch thick, and can either be sawed or planed down to this thickness. Cut tenons on the ends of the back rails (J and K) similar to the ones on the uprights, only across the thickness of the piece instead of with it (see detail); then lay out mortises on the inside edges of the rails for the back slats. These mortises need to

be only ¼ inch deep. Use a ⅜-inch bit with a depth stop to bore the waste from these mortises, and clean them out with a sharp chisel.

10. Assembling the back

Cut the lower ends of the back uprights (L) at a 15° angle. Dry-assemble the back rails and slats, and hold the assembly up to the back uprights to mark the positions of the mortises that will hold the tenons of the back rails. Position the upper rail ¾ inch below the tops of the uprights; the space between rails is 10¾ inches. Use a ¾-inch forstner bit, or if you don't have one, a smaller bit with a depth stop, to bore out as much of the waste for the mortises as possible, then square them out with a chisel. When everything fits, apply glue to the tenons, the ends of the back slats, and the insides of all the mortises, and clamp the assembly together. Thoroughly wipe away any excess glue with a damp rag and set the back aside to dry.

Arm Pattern

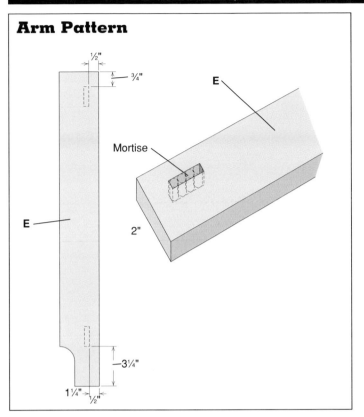

Side View

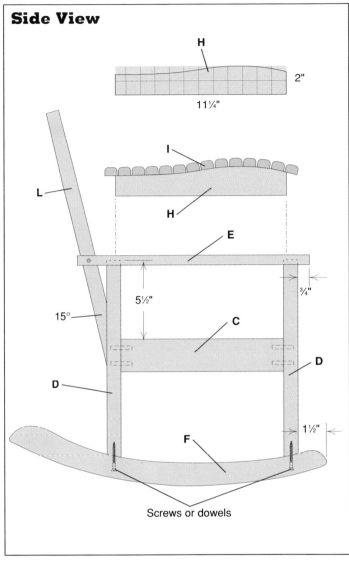

Screws or dowels

11. Attaching the back

After the glue has set up overnight, attach the assembled back to the back rail with one 1½-inch by #10 screw through each upright and into the seat support pieces. Attach it to each armrest with one screw. The screws should be countersunk and covered with "button" plugs.

12. Completing the seat

Crosscut 2 pieces of 1×6 material to 14 inches. Set up a quarter-rounding bit in a router, set the router in a router table, and round over all 4 long edges of each 1×6 piece. On a table saw, rip one ½-inch-thick slat (I) off each rounded edge. Repeat this process until enough slats have been cut for the seat. Sand them carefully to remove all saw and machine marks. Position the slats on the seat sup-

ports so that the front slat is almost flush with the front rail. The slats will have to be individually trimmed to length as they are nailed in place because the seat is narrower at the back. One brass nail in each end of each slat will complete the piece.

Using Dowels

Dowels are used for two purposes: as exposed structural members or as invisible reinforcements for joints. Most lumberyards and many hardware stores have dowels for both uses.

Dowels for structural use are smooth and are commonly sold in various widths and in 3-foot or 4-foot lengths. Dowels used for

joinery, called dowel pins, have longitudinal or spiral grooves that allow the glue to flow freely and let air escape when a glued joint is clamped. Dowel pins come in various lengths and widths and usually have chamfered ends, to make it easy to insert them into drilled holes in the joints.

If you purchase uncut dowel stock for joinery and the fit is very tight in the predrilled holes (from swelling), you will need to slim the dowel stock to avoid splitting the wood into which the dowels are inserted. To do this, drive the dowel stock through a sizer, sand it, or dry it in an oven set on low heat until it shrinks.

PLYWOOD TULIP CHAIR

This imaginative chair will add charm to any room, and it is simple to build using ¾-inch 13-lamination Baltic or Finnish plywood. You can use your imagination and this basic technique to create your own variation on this stylized-tulip design.

Materials List

Dimensions are finished size (in inches). Dimensions for curved piece are for stock from which piece is cut.

Part	Qty.	Description	Size/Material
A	1	Seat back	¾ × 19½ × 21 Baltic plywood
B	1	Leg	¾ × 17 × 24 Baltic plywood
C	1	Leg	¾ × 17 × 24 Baltic plywood
D	2	Arms	¾ × 6 × 17½ Baltic plywood
E	1	Seat	¾ × 16 × 20 Baltic plywood

Hardware

19 flat-head wood screws (2" × #10)
⅜" tapered plugs

Tools required are a saber saw (jigsaw); a portable circular saw; a router and round-over bit; and a drill with a pilot-hole cutter and a Phillips screwdriver bit. A disk grinder and two short bar clamps will also be helpful.

Baltic or Finnish birch plywood is used for this project because of its superior quality. Its wood layers have no voids, so the edges will be free of gaps. Also, after priming, the edges will take paint very evenly without showing through. One sheet is enough for two chairs.

1. Cutting the pieces

Expand the patterns for all the pieces and lay them out on a sheet of plywood, positioning them for the most efficient use of material. There should be sufficient room that you do not have to butt edges together or position the pieces in an interlocking arrangement. The direction of the grain is unimportant.

Use a saber saw to cut out the seat back (A), the legs (B and C), and the 2 arms (D). The seat (E) can be rough-cut with the saber saw, but a portable circular saw or a table saw should be used to bevel its back edge at a 6-degree angle. This bevel allows the back piece to tilt backward

at a comfortable angle. If you use a portable circular saw, clamp a straight piece of scrap lumber to the seat to act as a guide for the saw, set the saw

Exploded View

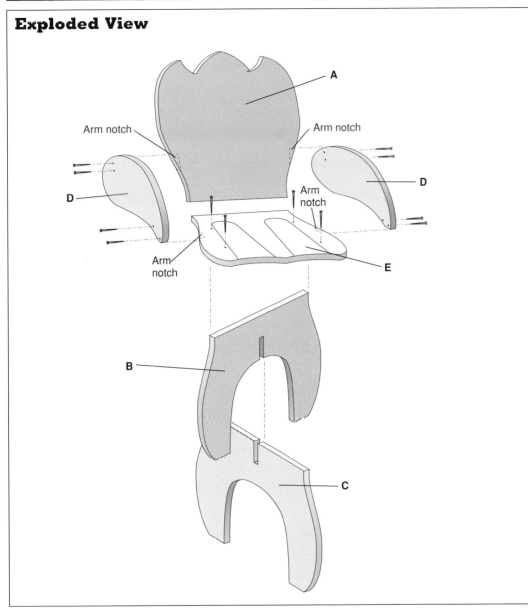

Arm notch

Arm notch

D

D

Arm
notch

Arm
notch

A

D

E

B

C

and counterbore for 5 screws at 3-inch intervals along the bottom edge of the back. Unclamp the 2 pieces and apply a coat of glue to the back edge of the seat; then reposition the pieces and insert the 2-inch by #10 screws. Put a drop of glue in each counterbore hole and tap a tapered plug into each. Thoroughly wipe away all excess glue before setting the assembly aside to dry. After the glue has dried, use a chisel, rasp, or grinder to cut the plugs down flush with the surface of the piece. Although the joint is very strong, you should handle the seat-and-back assembly carefully until the chair is completed and the arms are attached.

4. Attaching the legs

Spread a light coating of glue inside the notch of each leg and join the leg pieces so that their half-lap joints interlock. Use a square to be sure that they are at right angles to each other; then set them aside.

When the glue has dried, position the seat and back assembly on top of the legs. When you are satisfied with the seat position, draw lines around the leg tops on the underside of the seat, and place the seat upside down on a workbench. Use an ⅛-inch bit to drill pilot holes up through the seat bottom; use 2 screws in each leg piece. Now spread glue on the top edges of the legs, reposition the seat on the legs, and, with the pilot-hole cutter, drill back down through the holes you just made to make a counterbore in the seat and the pilot hole in the leg. Insert screws

at a 6-degree angle, and make the cut so that the top side is longest.

2. Rounding the edges

Use a ⅜-inch-radius round-over or quarter-rounding bit in a router to round over the edges of all the pieces, except where the seat and seat back will be joined, where the legs will interlock, and along the top edge of the legs. Use rasps,

a drum sander, a disk grinder, or whatever tool you have available to clean up and smooth out the curves you cut with the saber saw. Go back over the edges with the router and round-over bit again.

If you want to add depressions in the seat for more comfortable sitting, use the expanded pattern to trace guidelines. Using a disk grinder or a power drill with a sanding disk, make several passes

within the guidelines. Hold the disk at a slight angle at the outside edges of each depression, then increase the angle gradually as you move the disk toward the center.

3. Attaching the back to the seat

Use short bar clamps to hold the seat back in position with its bottom edge flush with the bottom surface of the seat. Using a pilot-hole cutter, drill

27

Patterns for Seat and Back

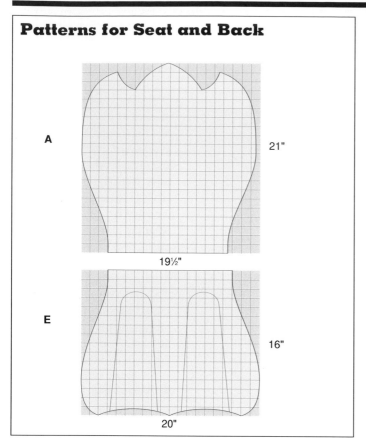

A — 21" — 19½"

E — 16" — 20"

Patterns for Legs and Arms

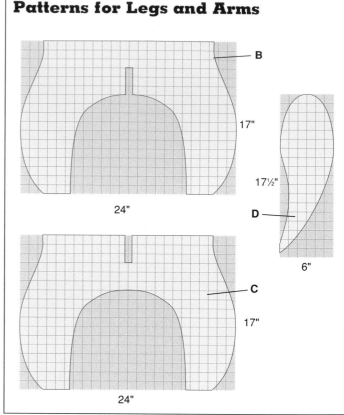

B — 17" — 24"

C — 17" — 24"

D — 17½" — 6"

down through the seat into the legs, tighten the screws, and plug the holes as before. Cut the plugs down flush after the glue has dried.

5. Attaching the arms

Now you need to cut notches in the seat and back where the arms will attach. This is a trial-and-error process. Hold one arm in position on the side of the chair, and mark its edges on the edge of the seat and seat back. Because the back piece is curved, the depth of the notch will vary. To mark the depth on the chair back, with the arm in place, hold a scrap of ¾-inch material against it. Scribe a line against the edge of the scrap. The notch on the back is about ¾ inch wide at the top, running

out to nothing at the bottom. On the seat, the notch is wider at the front than at the back. Mark the cuts for the notches on both sides of the back and seat, then use a handsaw or saber saw and a rasp or grinder to notch these areas. Trial-fit and trim until the arms will make tight contact all the way across. Since the chair is being painted, body putty can be used to fill cracks or holes if the notches were cut too large. Screw the arms to the chair with 2 screws in the seat and 2 in the back; plug the screwheads.

Sand the entire piece, apply at least one coat of primer, and paint with enamel colors of your choice.

Plywood for Wood Projects

Plywood is suitable for projects where large panels are required, or where the cross-bonding of the layers is an advantage. It is not prone to cracking or splitting along the grain, to warping, or to expansion and contraction due to changes in humidity. It can also be cut into intricate shapes without danger of splits or breakage.

Cheaper grades of plywood are made with Douglas fir or mahogany. Better grades have attractive outside veneers laminated to less expensive interior plies. The interior plies are coarse and have voids, or empty spaces,

that show as gaps along the edges of the plywood.

Premium plywoods, which have more laminations and no voids, are available through specialty lumber dealers. These plywoods include Finnish, or Baltic, birch and domestically produced maple plywoods. The birch plywoods are sold in 5-feet-square sheets and have more plies than other plywoods. As a result, Baltic birch plywood is dense, strong, stable, and able to hold an edge with negligible splintering or chipping. The surface veneers lack rich or exotic grain patterns, but take paint very well.

GATELEG TABLE

This beautiful small table is reminiscent of the simple elegance of Early American Shaker furniture. With one or both leaves folded down, it makes an attractive side or hall table; with both leaves up, it's the perfect size for a card or game table. The construction is simple yet sturdy, guaranteeing good service for years to come.

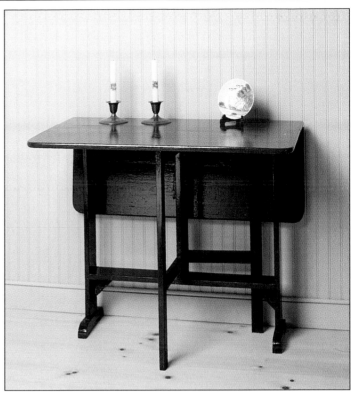

Tools required are a table saw or radial arm saw; a saber saw (jigsaw), band saw, coping saw, or router; a doweling jig; a drill with a ⅜-inch bit; and some lightweight bar clamps. A jointer, a pilot-hole cutter, and a Phillips screwdriver bit will also be handy.

Pine is a fine wood for this project, and will enhance the country look of the table. Oak or cherry would also work well and would be harmonious with the traditional nature of the piece.

1. Fabricating the top

Select the straightest wide stock for the top. You may be able to get the center piece (A) from a wide board without edge-joining, but the 2 leaves (B), which are 13½ inches by 35 inches, will probably have to be made by edge-joining 2 or more pieces. Cut the pieces roughly to length, then joint the edges that are to be joined. First lay the pieces out as they will go, and mark across the joints near both ends and in the middle for the dowel pins that will hold the pieces together. Use a doweling jig

to drill the ⅜-inch by 2-inch holes for the dowel pins, brush glue evenly onto both meeting edges and the dowel pins and in the holes, and insert the dowel pins. Use 3 or 4 bar clamps (see page 88) on alternate sides of the assembly to press the pieces together and hold them until the glue dries. Thoroughly wipe away any excess glue with a damp rag, and check with a straightedge to be sure that the assembly is flat. If you have a plate joiner, an alternative way to join the boards is to cut slots with it and glue wooden biscuits (flat wafers used instead of dowel pins) into them.

2. Assembling the gates

While the glue dries, rip and cut to length the pieces for the end legs (C), the gate frames (D, E, and F), and the horizontal stringer (G). Lay out the frames on a work surface. The horizontal pieces (F) should abut the short verticals (E) 1½ inches in from each end. The top horizontal should abut the long vertical (D) 1½ inches from the top. Mark across these joints for the ⅜-inch by 2-inch dowel pins, and use the doweling jig to drill the holes. Brush glue on the meeting surfaces and dowel pins

and in the holes before inserting the dowel pins, and clamp the frame together with bar clamps. Thoroughly wipe away any excess glue with a damp rag. Check for straightness and set the frames aside.

3. Cutting the feet

Cut the feet (H). The radius for the curved cut at each end is 2 inches, measured from a point along the bottom 2 inches in from the end. The void at the bottom of each foot is ¾ inch high and 5 inches long at the base, with ¾-inch-radius curves at each end. Use a sander to remove saw marks from the curved cuts. It is important that the tops of the feet be flat where the end legs will land on them.

4. Cutting dadoes in the legs

The end legs have horizontal dadoes to hold the horizontal stringer. Cut the dadoes 6 inches above the bottom edge of each leg, ¾ inch wide and ¼ inch deep, using a router or repeated cuts on a table saw or radial arm saw. Dado cutters tend to tear out the wood at the end of the cut when cutting across the grain, so they are not recommended for this cut (where both ends are exposed).

5. Boring holes for the leg dowels

Next drill holes for the dowel pins on which the gates rotate. To do this, make a jig from a piece of 1-by material of the same length and width as the horizontal stringer. At the midpoint of this board, draw a line across it at right angles

Exploded View

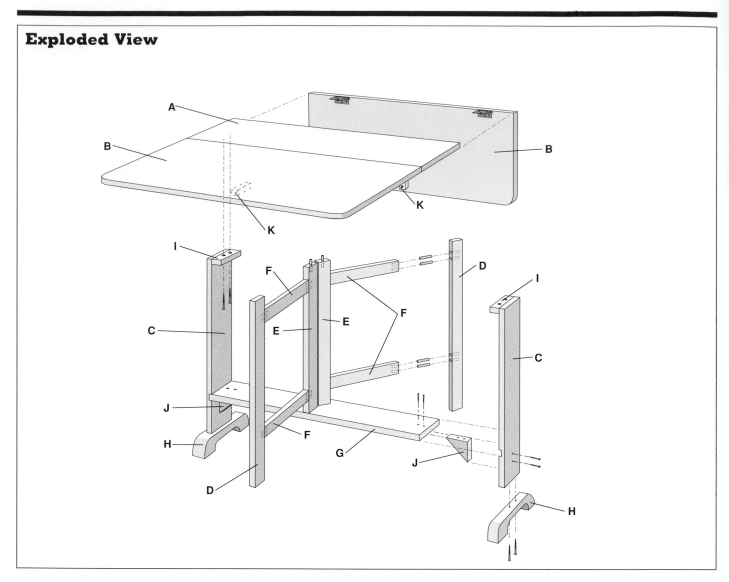

to its edge. Locate the hole centers on this line, ¾ inch in from either edge. Drill ¹³/₃₂-inch holes through the board at both of these points, and position the jig on the upper side of the horizontal stringer. Using the holes in the jig as a guide, drill holes of the same diameter ½ inch deep into the stringer. Use a depth stop like the one shown on page 85 to keep the bit from going all the way through. Now position the jig on the bottom of the center top piece of the table, centered from side to side

and end to end, and drill ¹³/₃₂-inch holes ½ inch deep into the underside of the top.

6. Attaching the end legs to the stringer

Assemble the end legs and stringer, using glue in the dado and 6d finishing nails through the legs and into the ends of the stringer. With glue and counterbored 1¼-inch by #8 screws, attach the triangular braces (J) to the underside of the stringer and the legs.

Plug the screw holes; when the glue dries, chisel and/or sand the plugs down flush. Attach the feet to the ends of the legs with 2½-inch by #10 screws, 2 in each foot.

7. Inserting dowel pins into the gatelegs

Mark the centers of both ends of the short verticals on the gate assemblies and use the doweling jig to drill holes for ⅜-inch dowel pins. Insert the dowel pins, lightly glued, and trim them so that they protrude no more than ⁷/₁₆ inch

from the end of the vertical. Slightly round the ends of the dowels slightly with sandpaper. Cut the 2 glue blocks (I) and the 2 stop blocks (K) and have them ready.

8. Assembling the table

Before proceeding with assembly, use 100-grit sandpaper either by hand or in an orbital sander to remove all work marks and to slightly round all the hard corners. Then paint or stain the tabletop,

Materials List

Dimensions are finished size (in inches). Dimensions for shaped pieces are for stock from which piece is cut.

Part	Qty.	Description	Size/Material
A	1	Center top piece	¾ × 7½ × 35 pine
B	2	Leaves joined from 1-by material	¾ × 13½ × 35 pine
C	2	End legs	¾ × 3¾ × 27½ pine
D	2	Long gate verticals	¾ × 1½ × 29¾ pine
E	2	Short gate verticals	¾ × 1½ × 21 pine
F	4	Gate horizontals	¾ × 1½ × 9 pine
G	1	Horizontal stringer	¾ × 3¾ × 27½ pine
H	2	Feet	1½ × 2 × 9 pine
I	2	Glue blocks	¾ × 1½ × 3¾ pine
J	2	Triangular braces	¾ × 3 × 3 pine
K	2	Stop blocks	¾ × ¾ × 3 pine

Hardware

2½" × #10 flat-head wood screws
1¼" × #8 flat-head wood screws
6d finishing nails
⅜" × 2" dowel pins
2 pairs butt or drop-leaf hinges

blocks, and leg assemblies and let them dry thoroughly (otherwise, the wet finish will interfere with the moving parts of the completed table). To assemble the table, glue and screw (with 1¼-inch by #8 screws) the glue blocks to the inside of the end legs, with the top edge of the blocks flush with the tops of the legs. Then turn the center top piece upside down on the workbench and center the leg assembly on it. Mark the positions of the legs, then drill pilot holes for screws through the glue blocks and into the tabletop. Lift the leg assembly enough to insert the dowel pins on the top ends of the gate verticals into the holes on the underside of the tabletop, then put the leg assembly in place and guide the dowel pins on the bottom ends of the

gate verticals into the holes in the stringer. Now glue and screw the glue blocks to the tabletop as before.

9. Attaching the leaves

Before attaching the leaves to the center top piece, trim them to length, sand them to even up the edge joint, then use a compass or a round object to mark the cuts for the rounded corners. Make these cuts with a saber saw, band saw, or coping saw, and use a router with a quarter-rounding bit to round over the edges that will be the outer edges of the finished table (don't round over the edges where the leaves meet the center piece). Sand and paint or stain the leaves and let them dry. To attach,

Adhesives for Woodworking

Most projects for interior use can be made with aliphatic (yellow) resin glue, also called yellow carpenter's glue, which is stronger and faster drying than polyvinyl acetate (white) glue. Aliphatic glue has the advantages of easy application and cleanup, as well as a quick set-up time. When properly applied, it forms a bond that is stronger than the wood (both bonding surfaces should be completely coated with a thin, even layer of glue), but it is flexible enough that the joined pieces can move a little (this is called "creep") over time. The quick set-up time (about 1 hour) can be a disadvantage for large, complicated assemblies, which are more easily put together with a urea-formaldehyde (exterior-grade) resin glue, which allows more time to work with the pieces.

Urea-formaldehyde resin glue, which is recommended for the exterior projects, is sold as a brown powder that must be mixed with water to form a glue with the consis-

tency of heavy cream. This glue sets in 6 to 12 hours depending on the temperature (see instructions on the can), and must be kept at a temperature of at least 70° F while drying. Urea-formaldehyde glues clean up with water. They are very hard and inflexible when allowed to dry properly.

None of these glues can be used to fill gaps. The joints where they are applied must fit tightly together. Pressure with bar or C-clamps must be applied to hold the workpieces tightly together until the glue dries. If gaps do occur in your joints, fill them with a putty-type filler or thin wedges of wood glued into place.

Contact cement is used for adhering thin veneers to various surfaces, such as exposed plywood edges. It must be applied to both meeting surfaces and allowed to dry until it's tacky before the surfaces can be joined. Then, once contact is made, the surfaces are instantly bonded and cannot be realigned.

use lightweight drop-leaf hinges or regular butt hinges. They can simply be screwed on without being mortised in. Position them about 3 inches in from each edge. A drop-leaf hinge has an offset pin (one leaf of the hinge is longer than the other) so that the crack between the table leaf and the center top piece will be open when the leaf is down.

With the gates fully open and the leaves up, mark the positions of the stop blocks (K), and glue and screw them to the bottom sides of the leaves with 1¼-inch by #8 screws. Touch up the finish, including the stop blocks, with oil, varnish, or paint.

TRESTLE KITCHEN TABLE

The trestle table is distinctive for its ancient lineage and simple but strong joinery. The version shown here, which has both Early American and modern elements, is 5 feet long and 29½ inches high and will seat six. The length can be varied according to need, but the top should project past each trestle by about a foot.

Tools required are a table saw or radial arm saw; band saw or saber saw (jigsaw); a drill; bar clamps; and sharp chisels. You may also want to use a router with a large quarter-rounding bit to shape the edges of the butcher block.

A hardwood is recommended for the support work of this table, since the top will be rather heavy. Bright-colored exotic hardwood will enhance the modern elements in the design, whereas a domestic wood such as oak or maple will emphasize its traditional aspects. Instead of the butcher-block top, less expensive material, such as plywood trimmed with solid wood edges, could be used, but the prefabricated butcher block greatly simplifies the construction.

1. Cutting the leg tenons

Cut the legs (B) from 8-inch or wider stock. Straighten one edge, then cut off both ends carefully so that they are square. The tenon on the bottom of the leg, which extends through the foot, is 2½ inches long, 6½ inches wide, and ½ inch thick. Mark the shoulder of the tenon 2½ inches up from the bottom end on all 4 faces of the leg. On the narrow edges of the leg, make a series

of ¾-inch-deep cuts with either a table saw or radial arm saw, working from the mark to the end. Then turn the piece flat and make ½-inch-deep cuts from the mark to the end. Now use a sharp wide chisel to remove the remaining waste on all 4 sides of the tenon. The repeated cuts will guide your depth and make the waste removal easy.

2. Shaping the leg

Narrow the upper part of each leg by making stopped ripping cuts on the table saw, or by making long straight cuts on a band saw or with a saber saw. If you use the band saw, use a hand plane to straighten the unevenness of the band-saw cut. The saber saw can be used to cut the curves at the bottom. Each of the decorative steps is 2 inches high and ½ inch wide, or you can vary the proportions to suit. Whatever saw is used, you will need to do some hand shaping and smoothing with a chisel, rasp, plane, and sander to remove work marks and refine the shapes.

Materials List

Dimensions are finished size (in inches). Dimensions for shaped pieces are for stock from which piece is cut.

Part	Qty.	Description	Size/Material
A	1	Top	1½ × 36 × 60 butcher block
B	2	Legs	1½ × 8 × 27 hardwood
C	2	Feet	1½ × 3½ × 27 hardwood
D	2	Top beams	1½ × 2 × 20 hardwood
E	1	Rail	1½ × 3½ × 38 hardwood
F	2	Wedges	½ × ¾ × 3½ hardwood

Hardware

8 drywall screws (2" × #10)
8 round-head screws (3" × #10), with washers
8 plugs

Exploded View

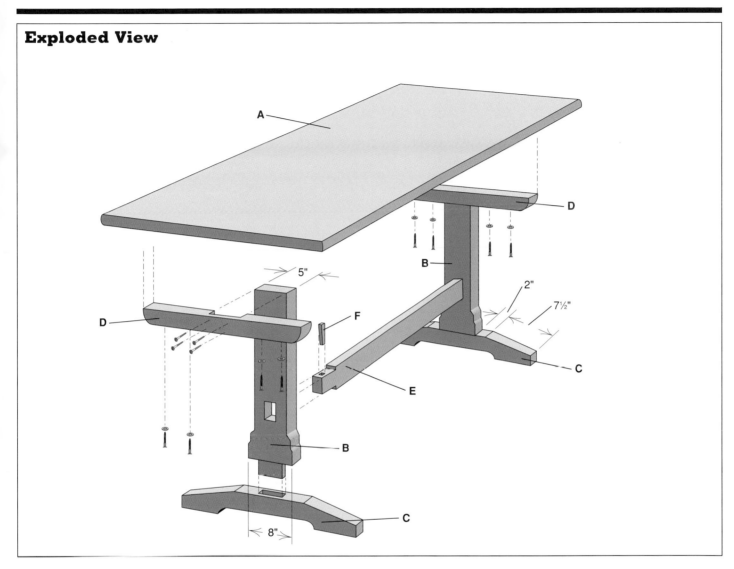

3. Cutting the leg mortises

Measure up 14 inches from the end of the tenon and let this be the bottom of the 1½-inch-wide by 2-inch-high mortise where the rail tenon comes through. Mark the mortise out carefully on both sides of each leg, and bore out as much of the waste as possible with drill bits. With a sharp ¾-inch or wider chisel, chop into the middle of the mortise along the lines that you have drawn. Work from both sides to avoid breaking out the wood around the edges.

4. Shaping the feet

Cut the feet (C). Cut out the bottom voids (1 inch high and 4 inches in from each end, with 1-inch-radius curves) with the band saw. Now cut the mortises for the leg tenons in the same manner as you cut the mortises in the legs. They are ½ inch wide by 6½ inches long, centered on top of the feet. Finally, cut the taper on the upper edges of the feet. The easiest way to do this is by marking the lines and cutting by hand on the band saw, but you can also make a simple tapering jig (see page 34) so that the taper can be cut on the table saw. When the tenons fit through the mortises and all cleanup work has been done on the parts, spread glue on all the meeting surfaces and clamp the feet onto the legs with bar clamps (see page 88) on either side of each leg. Check to be sure that the assemblies are square. Thoroughly wipe away any excess glue with a damp rag, then set the legs aside.

5. Attaching the beams

Cut the top beams (D). They have ½-inch-deep notches for the legs, to keep the table square. Cut these notches in the same way you made the tenons, with repeated cuts of the power saw. When the joints fit correctly, spread glue on the meeting surfaces, then clamp them together (making sure that they are square and flush). Use a pilot-hole cutter to counterbore screw holes for

Rail End

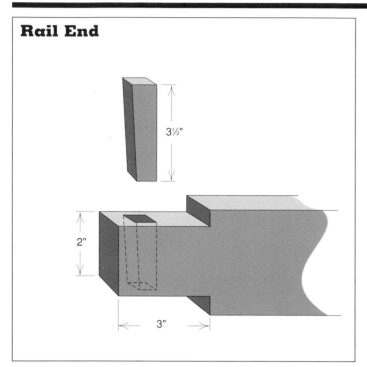

3½"

2"

3"

Rounding Edge of Table Top

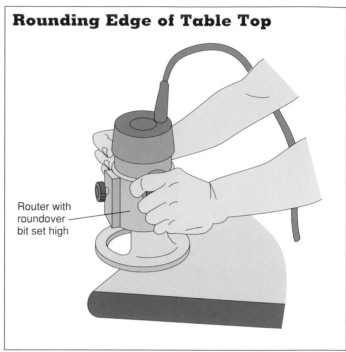

Router with
roundover
bit set high

Tapering Jig

Sawblade
path

This edge
glides against
saw fence

2"

7½"

¾" dowel

2"

5½"

2-inch by #10 screws (4 in
each leg). Insert the screws
and plug the counterbores;
after the glue dries, chisel and
sand the plugs flush.

6. Making the rail

Make the rail (E). It should be
22 inches shorter than the
length of the tabletop. Cut the
tenons on the ends like those
in the legs, but with shoulders
only on the top and bottom
edges, not on the sides (see
detail). Make the cuts 3 inches
in from the ends and ¾ inch
deep. When you have removed
the waste from the tenons, and
they fit through the mortises
in the legs, use a square to
make a line across the top edge
of each tenon 1½ inches from
the shoulder. Bore and chop a
½-inch-wide mortise vertically
through each tenon for the
wedge that will hold the leg
tight to the rail. Note that the
mortise starts ¾ inch long at the
top, but angles inward slightly

to follow the angle of the
wedge and to make it impos-
sible for the wedge to fall
through the mortise.

7. Cutting the wedges

Cut the wedges from ¾-inch-
thick stock. Rip the stock to ½
inch thick, then taper it from
¾ inch wide at the top to ½
inch wide at the bottom. This
angle should hold the wedge
tightly in place, so it won't
wiggle loose. If it does tend to
loosen, insert a small nail
through the bottom to hold it
tight, but make the nail easy
to remove so that you can
"knock down" the table.

8. Attaching the top

Lay the top upside down and
round the bottom edges, using
a router with a ¾-inch quarter-
rounding bit. You can achieve
a nice effect by setting the bit
high so that it doesn't make a
full quarter-round cut. You
could also round the edges by

hand with a plane and rasp.
Flip the top over and round
the upper edges the same
way. To attach the top, first
bore pilot holes through the
beams. They should be over-
sized so that the screws can
move as the tabletop expands

and contracts. Counterbore
the holes to conceal the screwheads and washers. Assemble
the frame. Then set the top in
place and secure it with 3-inch
by #10 screws and washers.

Sand and smooth all sur-
faces and apply an oil or varnish finish.

H ALL CLOCK

This simple but stately clock is an easy-to-build heirloom that will add a touch of timely elegance to any home. The pieces of the case are joined by dowels. In just a few minutes, you can make a jig to position the dowel holes. A standard doweling jig is used to join the frames for the doors.

Tools required are a planer; a table saw or radial arm saw; a saber saw (jigsaw); a drill or drill press with a ⅜-inch bit, an ⅛-inch bit, a pilot-hole cutter for #8 screws, and a 1⅜-inch (35mm) forstner bit; a doweling jig; several short bar clamps and C-clamps; and a router with a rabbeting bit and a special molding bit.

The most traditional wood for standing clocks such as this one is black walnut, but cherry, oak, or other dark hardwoods can also be used. If you select oak, you may want to stain it to help bring out the grain.

1. Cutting the case pieces

Select the boards for the 2 side pieces (A) carefully to be sure that they are straight and solid. You may need to joint one edge to straighten it before ripping the boards to width, and you will need to plane the boards down to the required 1¼-inch thickness. Cut the pieces to length. Then use a handsaw or jigsaw to cut the curved bottom of each side so that it has 2 feet, each about 1½ inches long. Use the rabbeting bit in the router to rout a rabbet along the back inside edge of each piece, ⅜ inch wide by ¼ inch deep (when viewed from the back).

Cut the bottom (B) and the top (C) pieces ¼ inch wider (6 inches) than the finished size. They will be trimmed later.

2. Making the doweling jig

To make a doweling jig for drilling the 24 holes needed to join the top and bottom pieces to the side pieces, cut a piece of ¾-inch stock 6 inches long by 1¼ inches wide (see illustration on page 36). Draw a centerline along the length of the 1¼-inch face and make 3 marks along it, at 1 inch, 2½ inches, and 4 inches from one end. With a drill press (for accurate alignment), drill a ⅜-inch-diameter hole through the stock at each mark. Next cut another piece of ¾-inch stock 1¼ inches wide by 3 inches long for the end piece. Screw it to the first piece at the end from which you measured the hole centers (so that the first hole is exactly 1 inch from the crosspiece). Check to be sure that the pieces are square and flush.

3. Drilling holes for the dowel pins

With a square, mark a pencil line across the inside face of each side piece 1½ inches down from the top. Clamp the doweling jig over one of the pencil lines with the end piece resting snugly against the back edge of the side piece and the pencil line centered inside the jig holes. Using a ⅜-inch bit with a depth stop, drill 3 holes 1 inch deep. Repeat for the other side piece. Now drill 3 bottom holes in the same manner, marking the guidelines 5 inches up from the bottom edge of each side piece.

Doweling Jig

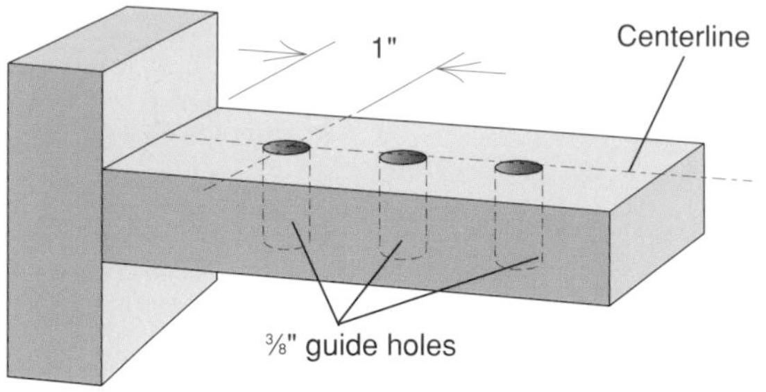

Next mark a centerline across one end of the top piece, clamp on the jig, and drill the holes. Be sure the crosspiece of the jig is pressed against the back edge of the top piece, so that all of the back holes will be exactly 1 inch from the back edge. Repeat for the other end of the top piece and both ends of the bottom.

Trim ¼ inch off the back edge of both the top and the bottom by rip-cutting them on a table saw, so that their back edges will be flush with the inside edge of the rabbets you have cut into the side pieces.

4. Assembling the case

Dry-assemble the case to be sure that everything fits; sand the dowel pins you use so that they will fit loosely for easy disassembly. When everything fits correctly, brush glue into all the holes, on the dowel pins, and on the ends of the top and bottom pieces. Insert ⅜-inch by 2-inch dowel pins, and use short bar clamps (see page 88) to bring the pieces together. Check for squareness, and then thoroughly wipe away any excess glue with a damp rag before setting the case aside to dry.

5. Making the door frames

Cut the pieces for the upper and lower doors (D, E, F, and G) to length and width. Be sure that the crosscuts on the rails (E and F) are made with a fine-toothed blade and are perfectly square in both directions. Lay the doors out on a workbench as they will go, and mark across the joints with a pencil and a square to indicate the dowel centers. Use an ordinary doweling jig and a ⅜-inch bit to drill the holes for the dowel pins. Brush glue into the holes and on the dowel pins and meeting surfaces, insert the dowel pins, and use short bar clamps to bring the pieces together. Check to be sure that the door frames are flat and square, then wipe away all excess glue before setting the frames aside to dry.

6. Hanging the door frames

When the door frames have dried, lay them on the workbench with their inside surfaces up. Use the router with the rabbeting bit to cut a ⅜-inch by ⅜-inch rabbet around the inside of each frame. Use a sharp ¾-inch chisel to square the corners of the rabbet where the router cutter leaves them rounded. Check to be sure that the door frames will fit properly in the case; if necessary, plane the edges of the frames to remove extra wood. When the fit is correct, use a 1⅜-inch forstner bit to bore holes into the frames for the concealed hinges. Center the holes 3 inches from the top and bottom edges of each frame, and 13/16 inch from the outside edge. Insert the hinges into the holes and attach them with the screws provided. To hang the door frames, screw the mounting block provided with each hinge to the inside of the side piece (A), slide the hinges into place, and tighten the set screw on each hinge. Check the door frames for fit; adjust them by loosening or tightening the hinge-adjusting screws. When the door frames are hanging properly, loosen the set screws and remove the door frames from the cabinet.

Materials List

Dimensions are finished size (in inches). Dimensions for shaped pieces are for stock from which piece is cut.

Part	Qty.	Description	Size/Material
A	2	Sides	1¼ X 7 X 62 hardwood
B	1	Bottom	¾ X 5¾ X 13¼ hardwood
C	1	Top	¾ X 5¾ X 13¼ hardwood
D	2	Upper door frame stiles	¾ X 1¾ X13 hardwood
E	3	Door rails for both doors	¾ X 1¾ X 9½ hardwood
F	1	Bottom door rail	¾ X 5½ X 9½ hardwood
G	2	Lower door frame stiles	¾ X 1¾ X 43 hardwood
H	1	Lower glass panel	⅛ X 10 X 36¼ glass
I	1	Upper glass panel	⅛ X 10 X 10 glass
J	2	Upper vertical stops	¼ X ¼ X 10¼ hardwood
K	4	Horizontal stops	¼ X ¼ X 10¼ hardwood
L	2	Lower vertical stops	¼ X ¼ X 36¼ hardwood
M	1	Movement mounting block	¾ X 3 X 13¾ hardwood
N	1	Back	¼ X 14 X 56 veneered plywood

Hardware

1 clock movement (Westminster Chime, Grandmother Movement; Stock #13001. Klockit Co., P.O. Box 636, Hyw. H North, Lake Geneva, WI 53147; 1-800-556-2548)
2 pairs concealed hinges (Gross #1002)
4 brass L brackets (1")
¾" brass nails
Brads
⅜" X 2" dowel pins
2 pinch or magnetic catches
2 door handles, if desired

Exploded View

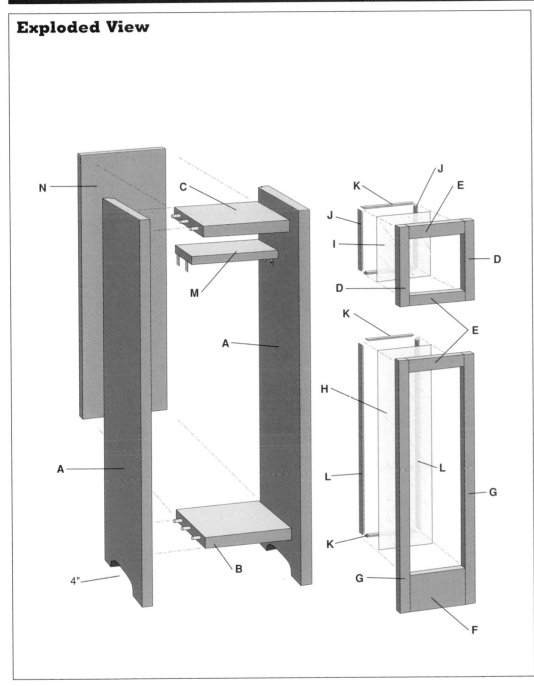

N

C

J

K

E

J

I

D

D

M

E

A

K

H

L

L

A

L

G

K

B

G

4"

F

8. Installing the clock mounting block

The clock movement will be attached to a mounting block (M). To position the mounting block, first screw the clock movement to it, then hold the block and movement in position so that the clock dial is aligned in the decorative metal clock face-framing piece and as close to it as possible without touching. Mark the position of the block on the case sides, then remove the block and detach the movement. Use 4 brass L brackets (1 inch) to attach the block to the case sides.

9. Installing the back piece

Measure the opening in the back of the cabinet to verify the dimensions of the back piece (N), then cut it. Make sure that the cabinet is square by measuring the diagonals, then attach the back with small brads.

10. Completing the clock

Carefully sand and apply finish to the entire piece. Hang the doors; attach pinch or magnetic catches to the case side opposite the hinges, and a handle on each door, if desired. Remount the movement on the mounting block according to instructions provided by the manufacturer. If you have a chiming or musical movement, you may want to drill some holes in the case side nearest it to make the sound more audible.

7. Finishing the doors

Sand the door frames thoroughly. Use an orbital sander to sand the flat areas, and hand-sand all the edges so that they are slightly rounded. Finish the frames with stain (if you wish) and varnish or oil.

Cut the stops (J, K, and L) for holding the glass in place; miter the ends of the stops. They should fit within the inset rabbeted into the door frames. With the frames facedown, set the glass panels (H and I) into the rabbets. Set the decorative metal face-framing piece that comes with the clock movement, and has a hole for the clock face, on the glass of the upper door. Lay the stops over the edges of the glass and metal pieces and nail them into the frame with ¾-inch brass nails, angled away from the glass.

37

This fancy mirror frame is surprisingly simple to build. You may use prefabricated moldings or make three of the moldings yourself; the other molding is available in home centers and lumberyards. The frame shown here features hand-painted wallpaper. You could also paint the wood; faux and sponge painting techniques can be particularly effective.

Tools required are a table saw; a miter box or power miter saw; a router and router molding bits; a drill with a ⅜-inch bit, a doweling jig, a pilot-hole cutter for #6 screws, and a Phillips screwdriver bit; a sander or hand plane; and several bar clamps.

If you are planning to paint the frame alder or poplar are inexpensive woods that will work for all the parts and will hold paint well. If you prefer a natural finish, pine or any hardwood could be used.

1. Cutting the frame pieces

Cut the 2 long frame pieces (A) and the 2 short frame pieces (B), with 45° angles (miters) on all the ends (the measurements listed are for the longest points on all the pieces).

Lay out the frame pieces as they will go, and make pencil marks across the joints to indicate the centers for the dowels that will hold the joints together. Use a doweling jig and a ⅜-inch bit to drill 2 holes in each end of each piece for the ⅜-inch by 2-inch dowel pins. Be careful not to drill too deep near the tapered ends of the frame pieces.

2. Gluing the frame

Brush glue into the holes and on the meeting surfaces and the dowel pins, insert the dowel pins, and begin working the joints together by tapping the pieces with a mallet. When all the pieces are on the dowel pins, apply bar clamps (see page 88) in both directions at each joint. Place the clamps for one direction behind the frame; place the clamps for the other direction at 90° to the first ones, and on top of the frame. Slowly bring the joints together by tightening a little in one direction, then a little in the other. Check for squareness. Thoroughly wipe away excess glue with a damp rag before setting the assembly aside to dry.

After the glue has dried, use a belt sander or hand plane on the side that will be the front, smoothing it completely. The other side of the frame can be left rough.

3. Attaching the bullnose and cove moldings

You can use prefabricated moldings or rout them from ½-inch by ½-inch stock with a cove-cutting bit. Cut the stock for the bullnose molding (C and D). Use a ⅜-inch-radius quarter-rounding bit in

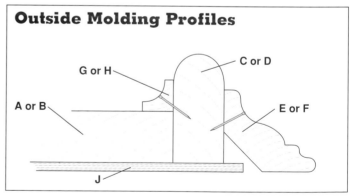

Outside Molding Profiles

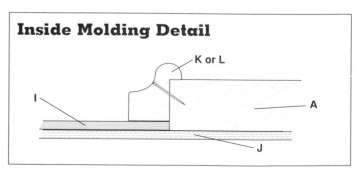

Inside Molding Detail

Materials List

Dimensions are finished size (in inches). Dimensions for shaped pieces are for stock from which piece is cut.

Part	Qty.	Description	Size/Material
A	2	Long frame pieces	¾ × 5 × 46 pine
B	2	Short frame pieces	¾ × 5 × 34 pine
C	2	Long bullnose moldings	¾ × 1¼ × 47½ pine
D	2	Short bullnose moldings	¾ × 1¼ × 35½ pine
E	2	Long crown moldings	⅝ × 1⅝ × 50 pine
F	2	Short crown moldings	⅝ × 1⅝ × 38 pine
G	2	Long cove moldings	½ × ½ × 46 pine
H	2	Short cove moldings	½ × ½ × 34 pine
I	1	Mirror	⅛ × 23⅞ × 35⅞ mirror
J	1	Mirror backing	⅛ × 36 × 48 plywood
K	2	Long inside moldings	⅝ × ⅞ × 36¼ pine
L	2	Short inside moldings	⅝ × ⅞ × 24¼ pine

Hardware

28 Phillips-head wood screws
½" × #6 heavy-duty picture-hanger wire
2 eye hooks (¾")
4d finishing nails
8 dowel pins (⅜" × 2")
Note: Paint-grade hardwood may be substituted for pine throughout.

Exploded View

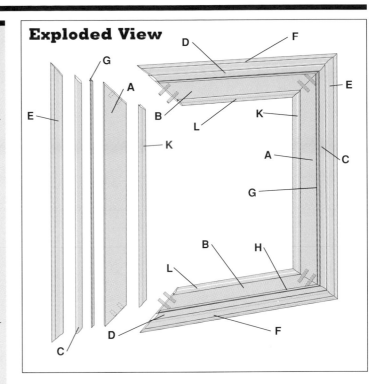

a router table to round both corners along one edge of each piece. Miter the pieces so that they will fit around the outside edges of the frame, then glue and nail them in place so that the square edge of the molding is flush with the back edge of the frame. Cut the inside cove moldings (G and H) to length, miter the ends, and glue and nail them to the frame inside the bullnose moldings.

4. Attaching the crown molding

The outer moldings (E and F) are a manufactured item called 1⅝-inch crown molding. This is a "sprung" molding, meaning that it is applied at an angle between 2 surfaces that are at right angles to each other. Here the molding is mitered, then glued and nailed around the outside of the bullnose moldings so that the outer edge of the frame appears to sweep back toward the wall. To make a compound miter cut with a table saw, set the miter gauge at 45° and hold the molding at a 45° angle to the saw table as you cut. If you use a power miter saw, hold the molding so that it leans at a 45° angle against the back fence, upside down. Use a sliding try square to draw a line on the outside of the bullnose molding where the inner edge of the crown molding will meet it. This line should be positioned so that the back surface of the crown molding will project past the back of the bullnose by ³⁄₁₆ inch. The ⅛-inch plywood mirror backing will fit into this gap.

Use 4d finishing nails to apply the crown molding; set the nails and putty over them.

5. Making the inside moldings

Rip the stock for the inside moldings (K and L). To shape them, with a router use a cove-cutting bit for the first pass and a half-rounding bit (or quarter-rounding bit in 2 passes) for the second pass, holding the molding upside down in a sprung position (at a 45° angle) for the second cut. Finally, cut a rabbet ⅛ inch wide by ⅝ inch deep (as viewed in cross section) along the outer edge with the table saw (see detail) to hold the mirror. Miter the ends of these pieces, then glue and nail them into place.

6. Painting the frame

The completed frame should be sanded, primed, and painted before the mirror is installed. Be sure to paint the back edges of the inside moldings because they will be visible in the mirror.

7. Installing the mirror

The mirror (I) fits into the rabbet formed by the inside moldings and the frame. Once you've set the mirror in place, cut the backing piece (J) to size, lay it over the mirror, and draw a line on it 6½ inches in from the outside edges, all the way around, to indicate the position of the mirror. Drill pilot holes for ½-inch by #6 screws 1 inch away from the mirror and 1 inch away from the outside edge of the frame on each of the 4 sides—4 pairs of screws on the long sides and 3 pairs on the short sides will be adequate. Insert the screws to hold the mirror and backing in place.

Use heavy-duty mirror- or picture-hanger wire and 2 eye hooks to hang the mirror.

STORAGE PIECES

This chapter features five storage pieces to help you organize almost any room in the home. Most of the projects are complex and will take several days to complete. Each of these projects includes at least one drawer. Because drawers offer a wide choice of joinery techniques, from simple butt joints to complicated dovetail joints, you can choose a style within your range of interests and abilities and still be able to complete the project successfully.

Each board of the elegant dovetail joint has a row of flared tenons that must be measured and cut precisely so the two pieces will interlock. Although a router and dovetail jig simplify the process of cutting these tenons—especially for multiple joints—you can certainly cut a few dovetails by hand with a backsaw and chisel. A simpler version of this joint is the finger joint, which has straight, not flared, tenons.

PLATE DISPLAY CABINET

This Early American–style piece is designed to show off your best china and add a touch of tradition to a dining room or kitchen. In a humble frontier home, the family's entire set of kitchenware would have fit on a wall rack such as this.

Tools required are a table saw or radial arm saw, a saber saw (jigsaw) or band saw, a miter box or power miter saw, a router with a ¾-inch straight cutting bit and a special molding bit, a drill, several bar clamps, a fine-toothed backsaw, and a chisel. A thickness planer would be handy.

This piece lends itself well to an elegant hardwood such as walnut or cherry, but pine would work for a more rustic look. The turned pegs and drawer pulls are available through specialty suppliers.

1. Cutting the side pieces

Cut the 2 side pieces (A) to length. Lay the pieces on a worktable with their inside faces up, their back edges together, and the tops and bottoms aligned. Measuring up from the bottom, make marks at 5 inches, 9¼ inches, and 22½ inches; also make a mark ¾ inch down from the top. Use a square to draw lines through these marks from edge to edge on both pieces, indicating the bottoms of the dadoes and the rabbet that will hold the shelves. Use a router with a ¾-inch straight cutting bit and a clamp-on straightedge to cut ¼-inch-deep dadoes based on all 4 of these lines. (An alternative dado technique, which produces the finer joints shown

in the photograph, is to cut the dadoes with a ½-inch bit and then cut ½-inch-wide tenons in the ends of the ¾-inch-wide shelves to fit into them.)

Next expand the pattern for the curved cuts at the bottom of the sides, transfer it to the side pieces, and cut these lines with a jigsaw. Sand and smooth the curved cuts and the insides of the side pieces.

2. Cutting the shelves

Cut the 4 shelf pieces (B). Lay the 2 bottom shelf pieces on the worktable with their back edges together and their better sides facing down. Measure in from each end 11¼ inches and draw a line across both pieces at this point, at right angles to the edges. These lines are the outside edges of the dadoes for the drawer dividers (C). Use the router and ½-inch straight cutting bit to cut ¼-inch-deep dadoes across both shelves at once. If you are using the optional dado technique shown in the photograph, cut ½-inch-wide tenons in the ends of all the shelves.

3. Assembling the cabinet

Plane a piece of ¾-inch stock to ½-inch thickness and check to be sure that it will fit in the slots in the shelves, then cut the 2 drawer divider pieces (C). Sand all the shelves and the

Exploded View

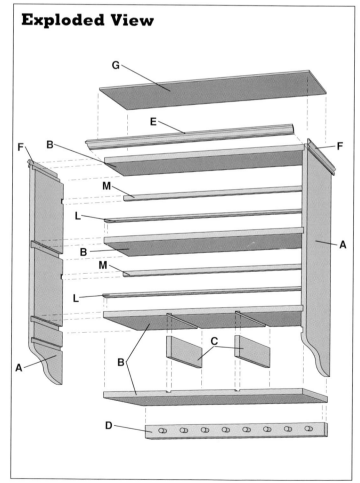

Materials List

Dimensions are finished size (in inches). Dimensions for shaped pieces are for stock from which piece is cut.

Part	Qty.	Description	Size/Material
A	2	Side pieces	¾ X 5½ X 36½ hardwood
B	4	Shelves	¾ X 5½ X 35¼ hardwood
C	2	Drawer dividers	¾ X 4 X 5¼ hardwood
D	1	Bottom stringer	½ X 3 X 34¾ hardwood
E	1	Long molding	¾ X 1½ X 37¾ hardwood
F	2	Short moldings	¾ X 1½ X 6¼ hardwood
G	1	Top cap	⅜ X 6¾ X 38¼ hardwood
H	3	Drawer fronts	½ X 3⅜ X 11⅛ hardwood*
I	6	Drawer sides	½ X 3⅜ X 5 hardwood*
J	3	Drawer backs	½ X 2⅞ X 11⅛ hardwood*
K	3	Drawer bottoms	¼ X 5 X 10⅝ plywood*
L	2	Plate-holder strips	¼ X ½ X 34¾ hardwood
M	2	Plate rails (optional)	¼ X ½ X 35¼ hardwood

Hardware

Brads, standard and brass

6d finishing nails

7–9 wood pegs

*Dimensions for drawer pieces depend on final opening size and type of joinery.

Pattern for Side

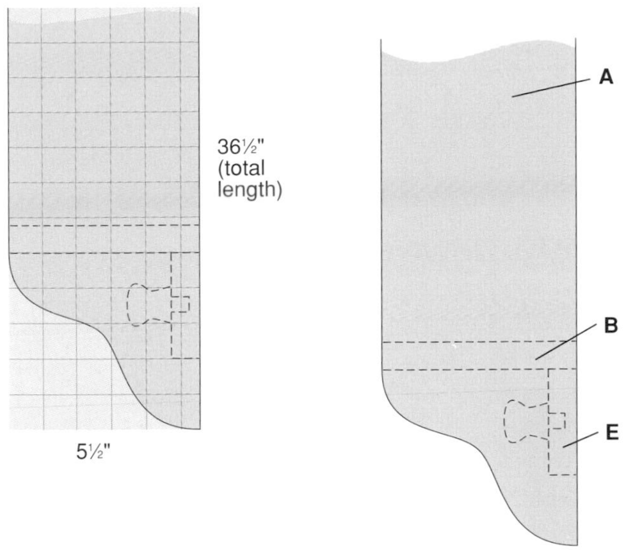
36½"
(total
length)
5½"
A
B
E

drawer dividers. Brush glue into the drawer divider slots and use bar or C-clamps to clamp the shelves to the dividers (see page 88). Thoroughly wipe away excess glue with a damp rag, then check to be sure that the pieces are square. After the glue has dried on the dividers, brush glue into the dadoes in the side pieces and assemble the case, using bar clamps to bring the pieces together and hold them while the glue dries. The shelves should all be flush with the front edge of the side pieces. Finishing nails may be driven through the sides into the ends of the shelves for strength if you are short of clamps. Again, wipe away excess glue, and check to be sure that the assembly is square before setting it aside to dry.

4. Attaching the bottom stringer

Cut the bottom stringer (D) to size and lay out centers for 7 to 9 pegs, depending on the size of your cups and the spacing you desire. Drill the holes, wipe a bit of glue on the tenons on the ends of the pegs, and insert the pegs; then apply glue to the top edge of the stringer and place it so that it is flush with the back edge of the side pieces (see detail). A couple of 6d finishing nails may be driven through the sides and into the ends of this stringer.

5. Attaching the moldings

You can use prefabricated moldings (E and F) for the top of the piece if the type of wood matches the cabinet, or you can make moldings with one of several router bits that are available for this purpose through specialty woodworking stores. Use a miter box or power miter saw to cut the front corners at 45° angles and to cut the back ends of the moldings square and flush with the backs of the side pieces. Glue and nail the moldings in place so that the bottom edge of the long piece is flush with the bottom of the top shelf.

6. Attaching the top

Plane or resaw a piece of 1x8 material down to ⅜ inch thick for the top cap (G). Cut it to size and use the router with a ⅜-inch quarter-rounding bit to round over the bottom edge on 3 sides (not the back). Use small brads to nail it down to the moldings so that it overhangs them equally on the front and sides.

7. Making the drawers

Plane or saw the stock for the drawer fronts, sides, and backs (H, I, and J) to the thicknesses listed, then cut the pieces to size. Cut the drawer bottoms (K) from ¼-inch plywood. Make dovetail joints as shown, or use a simpler method (see page 90 or other projects—adjust dimensions accordingly).

8. Adding plate-holder strips

Cut the 2 plate-holder strips (L) and attach them with a little glue and small brass brads to the shelves about ½ inch from the front edges, to keep plates from sliding off the shelves. If desired, cut 2 more strips (M) for plate rails, which hold the backs of the plates off the wall. Cut ½-inch by ½-inch by ¼-inch notches into the back edges of the side pieces to let in the strips (the notches are blind—they do not go all the way through the side pieces); position the notches to fit the plates you will display. The piece can be finished naturally with a varnish or an oil, or painted in a faux style to create an antique look.

CHEST OF DRAWERS

This is a challenging project that incorporates both modern and traditional design and construction. The plywood case helps keep the lines simple. The drawers are made in traditional fashion, with dovetail joints and wood drawer guides. However, see the section on making drawers (page 90) or other projects for easier drawer techniques.

A complete array of cabinet-making tools and machinery will be needed for this project, including: a table saw or radial arm saw, a saber saw (jigsaw), a jointer, a router, a doweling jig, a drill, clamps, a ¼- or ½-inch chisel, a dovetail saw or small backsaw, and standard measuring and marking tools.

Any solid wood and matching plywood could be used for this project. Pine is an easy wood to work with when cutting dovetail joints, and helps emphasize the traditional lines of the piece. Quarter-inch pine, birch, or even mahogany plywood can be used for the back and drawer bottoms.

Materials List

Dimensions are finished size (in inches). Dimensions for shaped pieces are for stock from which piece is cut.

Part	Qty.	Description	Size/Material
A	2	Case sides	¾ × 18 × 51½ plywood
B	1	Case top	¾ × 18 × 40½ plywood
C	2	Side caps	¾ × 4 × 18 pine
D	2	Side bases	¾ × 4¼ × 18 pine
E	1	Case back	¼ × 40¾ × 53 plywood
F	1	Case top back	¾ × 4 × 40 pine
G	2	Face-frame stiles	¾ × 1¼ × 56¼ pine
H	1	Face-frame top rail	¾ × ¾ × 39 pine
I	1	Face-frame bottom rail	¾ × 4¼ × 39 pine
J	1	Case top edge banding	¾ × 1 × 42 pine
K	12	Drawer frame fronts and backs	¾ × 2 × 40 pine
L	12	Drawer frame sides	¾ × 2 × 14½ pine
M	12	Drawer guides	½ × ¾ × 17¾ pine
N	10	Large drawer sides	½ × 8½ × 18½ pine or plywood
O	5	Large drawer backs	½ × 8 × 38½ pine or plywood
P	5	Large drawer fronts	¾ × 8½ × 39 pine
Q	5	Large drawer bottoms	¼ × 18 × 38½ plywood
R	1	Small drawer front divider	¾ × 2 × 5¾ pine
S	1	Small drawer divider	¾ × 5 × 16½ pine
T	1	Small drawer center support	¾ × 2 × 14½ pine
U	4	Small drawer sides	½ × 5 × 18½ plywood
V	2	Small drawer backs	½ × 4½ × 18½ plywood
W	2	Small drawer fronts	¾ × 5 × 19⅛ pine
X	2	Small drawer bottoms	14 × 18 × 18½ plywood
Y	1	Back leg support	¾ × 3½ × 40 pine
Z	4	Glue blocks	¾ × ¾ × 3½ pine

Hardware

1¼" drywall screws
Brads
12 drawer pulls
1" × #8 flat-head wood screws
⅜" × 2" dowel pins
⅜" × 1½" dowel pins

1. Cutting the plywood sides and top

Cut the sides (A) and the top (B). Cut a rabbet ¼ inch deep by ⅜ inch wide (when viewed from the back) along the back inside edges of all these pieces. Also cut a rabbet ¼ inch by ¼ inch along the top inside edges of each side piece.

2. Preparing the side caps and base pieces

Cut the side caps (C) and base pieces (D) from solid pine. Then expand and transfer the

Exploded View

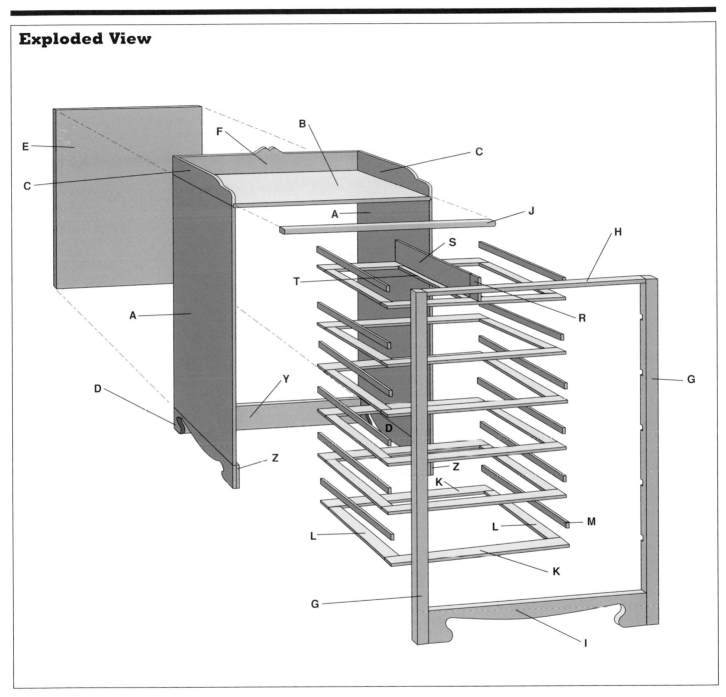

patterns for their profiles to the pieces, but don't cut them yet. Cut ½-inch-wide by ¼-inch-deep rabbets along the bottom inside edge of both cap pieces. These rabbets combine with the ¼-inch deep by ¼-inch rabbets on the top of the side pieces to form a dado approxi-

mately ¾ inch wide, which will hold the top; however, the width of the rabbets in (C) will depend on the exact width of the rabbets in (A) as well as the exact thickness of the ¾-inch plywood top (not always exactly ¾ inch), so make the necessary adjustments.

3. Assembling the sides

When you are sure that the top will fit in the rabbeted caps and side pieces, the side cap and base pieces can be edge-glued to the side pieces. Apply an even coat of glue to the meeting edges and use bar clamps (see page 88) to clamp

the pieces together while the glue dries. Be sure that the ends of the solid wood pieces are flush with or slightly overhanging the edges of the sides and that they conceal the edges of the plywood, especially on the outside. Thoroughly wipe away all excess glue with a wet rag, and use a straightedge to be sure that the glued-on pieces are straight with the plywood sides before setting the assemblies aside to dry.

4. Cutting the side cap and base pieces

When the glue has dried, plane and sand the surface of the solid wood so that it is flush with the plywood. Now use a saber saw to cut the patterns marked on the solid-wood pieces (you may need to remark them). After rough-cutting, use a router with a ⅜-inch quarter-rounding bit to round both sides of the exposed edges and curves, stopping the round-over on the inside of the cap piece about 1 inch from the back end, where the top back (F) will fit, and at the front edge about 1 inch from the bottom corner, where the top edge banding (J) will be applied. Use a rasp or small drum sander to smooth the edges and straighten any unevenness in the saw cuts. Go back with the quarter-rounding bit once more, then finally hand-sand to refine the edges.

5. Assembling the case

Cut some scraps to 40-inch lengths to lightly clamp between the lower ends of the sides—front and back—to hold the sides parallel while the glue dries. Brush glue into the dadoes and onto the ends of the top. Use bar clamps to bring the pieces and 40-inch spacers together. Wipe away all excess glue, and measure the diagonals to be sure that the piece is square. Tack diagonal braces to the edges or

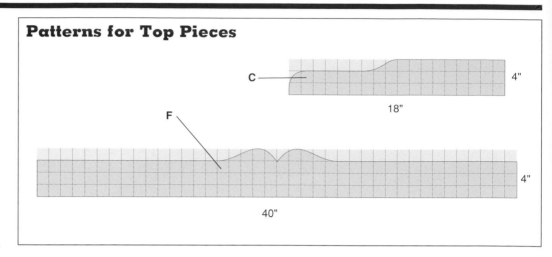

Patterns for Top Pieces

Patterns for Bottom Pieces

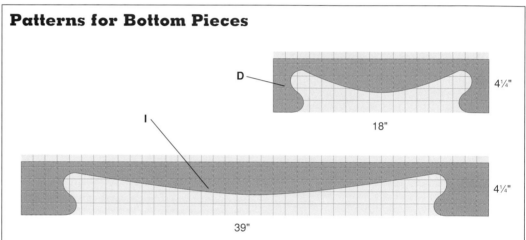

wedge them inside the piece to square it up if necessary.

While the glue is drying, cut the back top piece (F). First rip the piece to width, then hold it in place and mark where the tops of the cap pieces intersect its ends; expand and transfer the pattern accordingly. Make the cuts with a jigsaw or band saw, refining the curves as for the side cap and base pieces. Apply glue to both ends and the bottom edge of the back top piece. Use C-clamps and a bar clamp to hold it to the top and cap pieces while the glue dries.

6. Cutting the face-frame pieces

Cut the face-frame stiles (G) and top rail (H). Cut the bottom rail (I) to length and width, expand and transfer the pattern, and cut and round this piece in the same manner as for the side caps.

Make a special jig for cutting the dovetails on the inside edges of the face-frame stiles (see opposite page). Nail a 12-inch scrap of 1x1 to the edge of a scrap of ½-inch plywood, with the strip extending past the edge of the plywood a distance equal to half the diameter of the router base.

To lay out the dovetails, lay one of the stiles facedown and position the bottom rail as it will go, with both pieces flush at the bottom. On the back side of the stile mark the position of the top edge of the rail. Measure up 8⅞ inches from this mark and make another mark. Then measure up 9¼ inches for each of the next 4 marks. The last mark should be 6⅛ inches below the top edge, which will leave a 5-inch space for the top drawer. These 5 marks on the back of the stile will guide placement of the jig for cutting the dovetails on the inside edges. To make the cuts, clamp the 2 stiles together with their ends

Drawer Frame and Face Frame Details

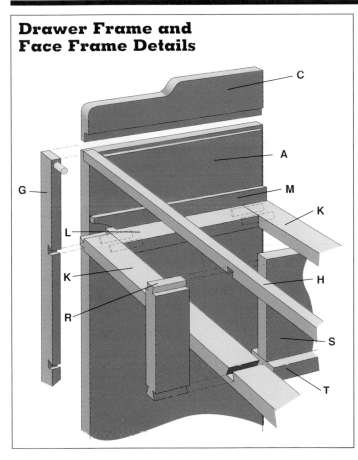

Cutting Dovetails in Face Frame Pieces

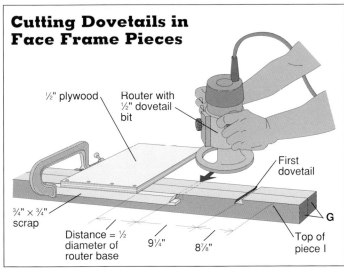

½" plywood

Router with ½" dovetail bit

First dovetail

¾" × ¾" scrap

Distance = ½ diameter of router base

9¼"

8⅞"

Top of piece I

G

flush and faces together and clamp the jig in position to guide the router (see above). Align the end of the 1x1 with the center of the first mark on the back of the stile, and use the plywood edge to guide

the router base while you make the dovetail cut through both stiles at once. Use a standard ½-inch dovetail cutter in the router, and set it to cut the dadoes ½ inch deep.

Cut a dovetail dado into the center of the bottom edge of the top rail. To avoid weakening this thin stock too much, reset the depth of the dovetail cutter to ⅜ inch instead of ½ inch. This dado will hold the top of the small drawer front divider.

7. Assembling the face frame

Lay all 4 face-frame pieces on the workbench as they will go and mark across the joints for the dowel centers—one dowel pin in each top joint and 2 in each bottom joint. Use a doweling jig and a drill with a ⅜-inch bit to drill the holes for the dowel pins; then brush glue into the holes and onto the dowel pins and meeting surfaces, insert the ⅜-inch by 1½-inch dowel pins, and use bar clamps to bring the pieces together. Wipe away all excess glue, and use a straightedge to be sure that the assembly is flat before setting it aside to dry.

8. Attaching the top edge banding

Cut the case top edge banding (J), then use a ¼-inch round-over bit to round the outer edges and ends, but not the edge that will be glued to the case top. Glue the banding to the top; use bar clamps to hold the pieces together. Wipe away all excess glue while it is still wet. After it has dried, plane or sand the banding flush with the case top.

9. Attaching the face frame

Glue the face frame to the case. Check to be sure that it fits tightly against the front edges of the plywood, and that its top edge fits tightly against the underside of the top edge banding. Apply glue to the plywood edges and top edge of the face frame, and use bar clamps to hold the face frame against the sides. Be very careful to keep both the case sides and the face-frame stiles straight, so that the space between them (where the drawer frames will fit) is the same from top to bottom. C-clamps can be used to hold the top rail of the face frame against the underside of the case top.

10. Making the drawer frames

Cut the front and back pieces (K) and the side pieces (L). Five of the front pieces should have dovetail tenons cut into both ends, to fit into the dovetail dadoes in the face-frame stiles. Put the router in a router table, with the same dovetailing bit that you used to cut the dadoes. Clamp a fence to the tabletop so that just one edge of the bit protrudes from it (set the bit to the same height as before—½ inch), and with 2 passes on each end, cut dovetails on the ends (practice with a scrap piece to make sure that the dovetail fits snugly into the dovetail dadoes in the stiles). Do not cut tenons on the bottommost frame front—it should have square ends. Cut the small drawer front divider (R). Reset the height of the dovetailing bit to ⅜ inch and cut the shorter tenons on the ends of (R). Cut a corresponding dado in the top edge of the uppermost drawer frame front to hold the bottom of the front divider.

Now lay out the face frames as they will go, with the side pieces butting up to the inside edges of the front and back pieces, flush along the outsides. Make marks across the joints for the dowel pins (³⁄₈ inch by 2 inch) that will hold them together, 2 dowel pins at each joint. Drill holes for the dowel pins with the doweling jig, spread glue on the meeting surfaces and dowel pins and in the holes, and insert the dowel pins. Glue and clamp the frames together in the same manner as the face frame was assembled, being sure to wipe away excess glue; check for flatness with a straightedge.

11. Attaching the drawer frames

Rip ¾ inch off the front edge of the bottommost frame (the one that does not have dovetail tenons) on a table saw. This frame will be positioned behind the face-frame bottom rail (I) so that it is flush with the top edge of this rail. Apply glue to the front edge of this frame (where you just ripped it) and to the side edges. Use C-clamps to hold it to the face-frame rail and the insides of the case while the glue dries. Use a C-clamp to clamp the front edge to the face frame. Carefully check to be sure that the sides of the frame are square to the face frame, then clamp them to the case sides with C-clamps.

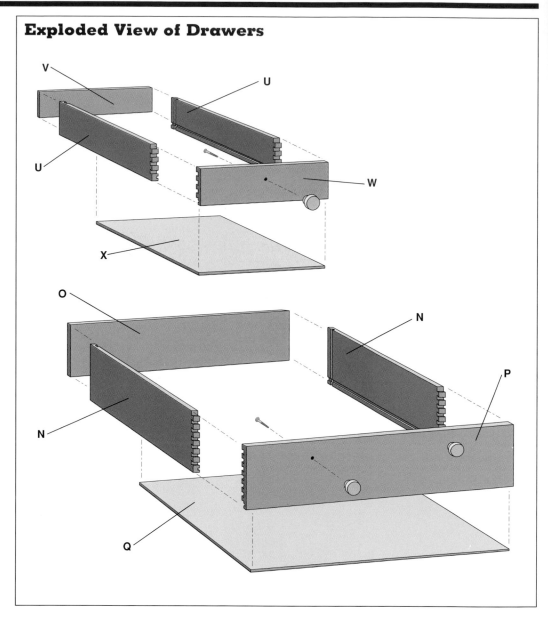

Exploded View of Drawers

Cut the back leg support (Y). Glue it in place flush with the rabbets in the back of the cabinet. Position the back edge flush with the back of the bottom drawer frame, which can be glued and nailed to it to help secure it. Cut the glue blocks (Z); glue and screw them inside all 4 corners to reinforce the joints between the side bases and the face-frame bottom rail, and the side bases and the back leg support.

Apply glue to the lowest dovetail dado and to the dovetail tenon on the next drawer frame. Also apply a thin coat of glue to the outside edges of the frame for about the last 6 inches near the back. Now slide the frame into place from the back, and work the tenons into the dovetail dadoes, being careful not to force them, which will break out the grain on the front of the face-frame stiles. When

the tenons are all the way into the dadoes (position them so that they protrude from the stiles slightly), check to be sure that the distance between the 2 drawer frames is the same at the back as the front, and clamp the back corners of the frame to the case sides with C-clamps. Insert the remaining frames in the same manner (you can use a board ripped to 8½ inches as a spacer between the frames). Work the small drawer front divider into place in the same way.

12. Attaching the drawer guides

Cut the drawer guides (M). These pieces will guide the side-to-side movement of the drawers, as well as add strength to the drawer-frame assemblies. Apply a thin coat of glue to one side and the bottom edge of each of these pieces, and use small 1-inch brads to nail them in place against the insides of the case sides and the tops of the drawer frames. Set the nails so that they won't scratch the drawers.

13. Installing the drawer divider

Cut the small drawer divider (S). Apply glue to the top edge and front end of the divider, and slide it into place behind the small drawer front divider (R). Check to be sure that it is perfectly parallel to the sides of the case, then use C-clamps and a light bar clamp to clamp it to the front piece and the case top. Wipe away all excess glue. Cut the small drawer center support (T). When the glue on the divider has dried, glue the support to the bottom of the divider. It fits between the front and back of the top drawer frame and supports the inner edges of both of the small drawers.

14. Making the drawers

Cut all the drawer pieces (N, O, P, Q, U, V, W, X). The fronts are made from ¾-inch pine. Make the sides and backs of the same pine planed down to a thickness of ½ inch, or use ½-inch plywood for the sides and backs. Cut a vertical dado (either dovetailed or ½-inch-wide square) ¼ inch deep on the inside surface of each drawer side (N and U) about ½ inch from the back edge to hold the drawer backs (O and V). Cut ¼-inch by ¼-inch square grooves, ¼ inch from the bottom on the bottom inside edges of all the sides and drawer fronts to hold the drawer bottoms (Q and X).

There are several types of joints you could use where the sides meet the fronts (see page 90, and other projects; adjust dimensions accordingly). If you wish to make hand-cut dovetail joints, use a marking gauge or square to mark a line across each drawer side ½ inch from the front edge and parallel to it. Lay out an even pattern of dovetails between the line you have drawn and the front edge. Make each dovetail ½ inch wide at its narrower end, ¾ inch wide at its wider end. Use a fine-toothed backsaw or dovetail saw to cut in along the lines, starting at the front edge. Keep the saw kerf on the waste side of the lines. Use a sharp chisel to chop out the waste. Don't cut past the line as you chisel.

To lay out the dovetail cuts for the drawer fronts, first draw a line across each end of the inside of each drawer face, ½ inch from the end and parallel to it. Next lay one of the drawer sides against the end of each drawer front, ¼ inch back from the drawer face, so that the back edge of the drawer front aligns with the deepest cuts on the side piece. Carefully trace the tails onto the end of the drawer front. With a square, extend the marks on the back of the drawer front to the line you drew. Repeat for the other side of each drawer. Put each drawer facedown on the workbench with the end you are working on toward you. Hold a saw at a 45° angle to the end and cut as far in as you can on the lines without sawing through to the face. Repeat for all the lines, then remove the waste wood by chiseling in from both the back and the end of each drawer front. Test the joints and pare wood out of tight areas until they fit together; cut wood away from the insides of the joints while leaving the outsides (where it will show) as tight as possible.

When the joints for the drawers fit together, brush glue (not too much) into the vertical dado and the meeting surfaces of the dovetails, and use short bar clamps to clamp them together. Check to be sure that each drawer is square and that the grooves for the bottom line up. The back piece should come down just flush to the top of the groove, so that the bottom can be slid in under it. When the glue is dry, slide the bottom into place and nail small brads from below into the bottom edge of the back.

When the drawers are all assembled, use the router to round-over the outer edges of the drawer fronts, and sandpaper to round the top edges of the sides and back. The dovetail joints can be sanded or planed to smooth them.

15. Completing the chest

Attach the handles or pulls and check the fit of each drawer. If they fit too tightly to work smoothly, you can remove wood from the inside surfaces of the drawer-frame top pieces, or the top edges of the drawers, but avoid removing too much wood. The drawers should fit as tightly as possible without binding. Paste wax can be applied to the drawer guides so that the drawers will slide more easily.

When all the drawers fit, and all work on the inside of the case is complete, cut the case back (E) and screw it into place in the rabbet. Drive 1-inch by #8 screws through the back and into the back edges of the case and into the backs of the drawer frames on each side—the drawers will stop against the back when they are closed and over time could loosen the back if it isn't securely fastened. The drawers should slide in just far enough to hide the joints, which means that they will protrude from the front of the case about ³⁄₁₆ to ¼ inch when closed.

Varnish or oil can be used to finish the outside surfaces of the piece.

EARLY AMERICAN ARMOIRE

*Armoires vary from the heavy, elaborate deco-
ration of medieval pieces to the spare grace of
Shaker pieces. This project, with its raised
panels and simple lines, is Early American in
style while incorporating modern materials—
plywood—to simplify its construction.*

Materials List

Dimensions are finished size (in inches).

Part	Qty.	Description	Size/Material
A	2	Sides	¾ × 13½ × 76 pine plywood
B	2	Case bevel pieces	¾ × 3½ × 76 pine
C	1	Bottom	¾ × 15 × 41 pine plywood
D	1	Fixed shelf	¾ × 15 × 41 pine plywood
E	2	Face-frame stiles	¾ × 2¼ × 76 pine
F	1	Face-frame top rail	¾ × 4½ × 32⅝ pine
G	1	Face-frame bottom rail	¾ × 10 × 32⅝ pine
H	1	Back stringer	¾ × 4 × 40½ pine
I	1	Shelf edge banding	¼ × ¾ × 32½
J	1	Top	¾ × 18 × 46 plywood
K	2	Side crown moldings	2¾ × 14¼ crown molding**
L	2	Bevel crown moldings	2¾ × 5⅛ crown molding**
M	1	Front crown molding	2¾ × 38½ crown molding**
N	2	Side half-round moldings	½ × 1 × 14½ half-round molding
O	2	Bevel half-round moldings	½ × 1 × 5½ half-round molding
P	1	Front half-round molding	½ × 1 × 38⅞ half-round molding
Q	2	Side base moldings	¾ × 3¼ × 14 pine
R	2	Bevel base moldings	¾ × 3¼ × 4¼ pine
S	1	Front base molding	¾ × 3¼ × 37¾ pine
T	4	Feet	1½ × 1½ × 9¾ hardwood
U	4	Door stiles	¾ × 3 × 62 pine
V	6	Door rails	¾ × 3 × 10⅞ pine
W	2	Lower panels	¾ × 11¼* × 19* pine
X	2	Upper panels	¾ × 11¼* × 35¾* pine
Y	1	Astragal	½ × 1¼ × 61½ pine
Z	1	Back	¼ × 41¼ × 72 plywood
AA	***	Adjustable shelves	¾ × 15 × 40¼ pine plywood

Hardware

⅜" × 2" dowel pins
4 cabinet hinges (⅜" offset)
Clip catch
Lock
Shelf clips
Small brads
6d finishing nails
*Approximate; measure frame before cutting.
**If you are not used to working with crown molding, you
may want to buy extra to allow for errors in cutting.
***Number of shelves depends on personal preference.

Tools required are a table saw; a portable circular saw or panel saw with a fine-toothed blade; a miter box or power miter saw; a drill with a ⅜-inch bit, a doweling jig, and a ¼-inch bit; a router with a ¾-inch straight cutting bit; lots of light bar clamps and C-clamps; and standard hand woodworking tools.

Like traditional American armoires and other furnishings, this armoire is made of pine boards because of the wood's availability and easy workability. The piece incorporates pine-veneered plywood for the sides, back, and shelves. Other woods and plywood veneers, such as oak, cherry, or birch, could also be used. Oak takes a stain nicely, whereas cherry is beautiful with just a clear finish. Birch is usually the most economical wood to use if you intend to paint the finished piece.

1. Cutting the side pieces

Cut the sides (A) from a full sheet of ¾-inch veneered plywood, first by cutting 20 inches off one end of the sheet with a portable circular saw, then by ripping the 2 sides, each 13½ inches wide, from the remaining 76-inch-long piece. Leave both long edges square for now. Rip the case bevel pieces (B). Leave their edges square for now as well.

With a table saw, or a router and rabbeting bit, cut a ¼-inch by ¼-inch rabbet along the back inside edge of both side pieces to hold the back.

2. Dadoing the side pieces

Lay the 2 side pieces on a workbench with their inside surfaces up and the rabbeted back edges touching. Flank them with the case bevel pieces, inside faces up also,

Exploded View

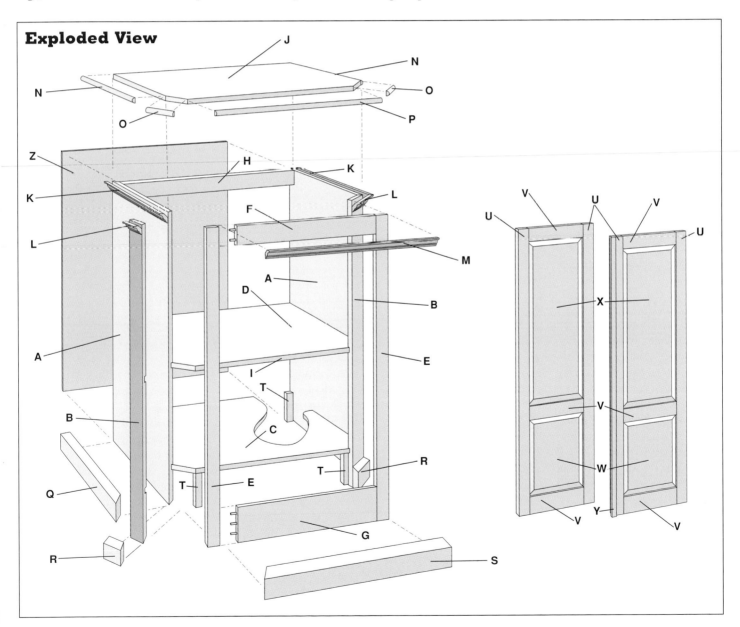

Molding and Door Sections

Attaching Molding Pieces

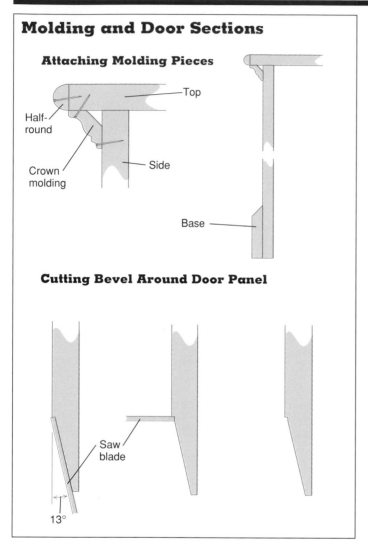

Cutting Bevel Around Door Panel

Left Door Detail

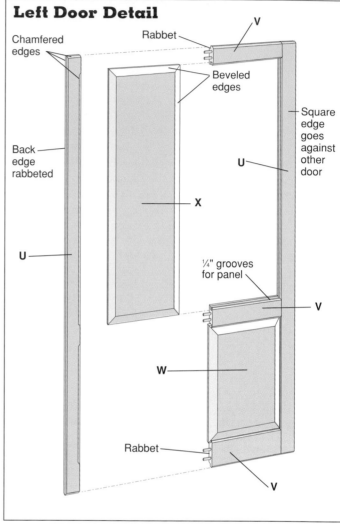

with all their bottom edges even. Measure up from the bottom edges 9¾ inches to mark the bottom edge of the dadoes that will hold the bottom. Draw a pencil line across all 4 pieces at this height. Use the router with a ¾-inch straight cutting bit and a clamp-on fence to cut this dado; it should be ¼ inch deep. If you line up the bottom edges of the 4 pieces carefully and use a short bar clamp at each edge to hold the guide and the pieces firmly to the workbench, you can make the dado through all 4 pieces in a single pass.

Repeat for the middle dado, the bottom of which is 40 inches from the bottom edge of each side. This dado will hold the fixed shelf.

3. Cutting the bottom and the shelf

Cut the bottom (C) and the fixed shelf (D). Use a bevel square to mark a line at a 45° angle to the 2 front corners of each piece. Start the line 2 inches from the corner on

each edge; it should be exactly 2¾ inches long. As you cut off each corner, keep the saw blade on the waste side of the line.

4. Cutting the face-frame pieces

Now cut the face-frame stiles (E), the top rail (F), and the bottom rail (G). Cut the rails an extra ¹⁄₁₆ inch to ⅛ inch long; you can trim them to exact length after dry-assembling the case. Leave the edges of the stiles square for now. The ends of the rails must be perfectly square in both directions

so that can be doweled tightly to the verticals.

Lay out the face-frame pieces out as they will go (with the top and bottom edges of the rails flush with the ends of the verticals), then mark the lines across the joints for the dowel centers. With a doweling jig, drill holes for ⅜-inch by 2-inch dowel pins. Check to be sure that the dowel pins fit easily into the holes (see page 86). Do not assemble the face frame yet.

5. Beveling the edges

Set the table-saw blade to cut a 22½° angle. For best results, use a 60-tooth carbide blade. Cut 22½° bevels on the front edges of the side pieces (A), both edges of the case bevel pieces (B), and the outside edges of the stiles (E). Be careful that you don't make 2 left- or right-side pieces—they must be mirror images of each other. Be sure that the bevel cuts do not trim the outside faces to narrower widths.

6. Gluing the side assemblies

To join the case bevel pieces to the sides and face-frame stiles, you will have to clamp in both directions at once. Cut some triangular pieces of scrap approximately 3½ inches by 2½ inches by 2½ inches (right triangles) to place temporarily against the case bevel pieces for the clamps to grip from both directions.

Position the bottom and the fixed shelf in their dadoes in the side pieces so that the back edges are flush with the rabbets in the side pieces (not the back edge). Next brush an even coat of glue on the beveled edges of one side piece, one case bevel piece, and the stile; position them together on one side of the case. Place a 3½-inch by 2½-inch by 2½-inch triangular scrap against the face of the side bevel piece and, using it as a toehold to clamp in 2 directions at once, clamp the stile to the scrap with a short clamp and the side piece to the scrap with a longer clamp (see page 88). Repeat with 2 or 3 more pairs of clamps and more scrap, then glue and clamp the

corresponding 3 pieces on the other side of the case. Thoroughly wipe away any excess glue with a damp rag. Check that all edges are aligned and tight. If necessary, bring and hold errant edges together with 6d finishing nails.

7. Assembling the case

For final assembly you will need 6 scraps of 2×2 (or 2×4), 16 inches long, and a helper. When the glue has dried on the side assemblies, but before unclamping them, check the distances between the inside edges of the face-frame stiles where the top and bottom rails will go; adjust the lengths of (F) and (G) as necessary. Cut the back stringer (H). Now unclamp the side assemblies from the bottom and the shelf. Brush glue into the holes for the dowel pins in the edges and ends of the face-frame pieces, into the dowel pins, and into the dadoes that will hold the shelf and the bottom. Brush an even coat of glue onto the front edge of the bottom so that it can be glued to the inside edge of the face-frame bottom rail.

Tap dowel pins into the ends of the face-frame rails, clamp the side pieces in position on the shelf and the bottom with one clamp at the back edge, and work the rails into place on the stiles. Clamp (but do not attach) the back stringer in place. Hold the 16-inch lengths of scrap horizontally across the sides where the shelf and the bottom are, and at the top, and hold them in place with 3 bar clamps across the back.

Now you can apply plenty of pressure to close the dowel joints between the face-frame rails and the stiles by bar-clamping from 2×2 to 2×2 across the front. Several light bar clamps should also be applied to hold the bottom rail tightly against the bottom (be sure that their top edges are flush). Check the diagonal measurements of the case to see that it is square.

8. Completing the case details

Once the glue has dried and the clamps have been removed, the joints can be sanded or planed lightly to smooth any unevenness. Cut the shelf edge banding (I); glue it in place and hold it with light bar clamps. Nail the back stringer permanently in place with 6d finishing nails. Its back face should be flush with the rabbets in the side pieces so that the back can overlap the stringer and be nailed to it. Set all nail heads and putty the holes.

9. Attaching the top

Cut out the top (J) a little larger than the size listed; leave all 4 corners square for now. Position it on top of the case so that the back edge is flush with the back of the case and the top hangs over an equal amount on both sides. Insert a couple of screws through the top into the stringer at the back and the face frame at the front to hold the top in place temporarily. Use a power miter saw or miter box to cut the 22½° angles on the crown-molding pieces (K, L, and M). The crown molding is a sprung molding, meaning

that it is applied at a 45° angle to the case and top. Hold a piece of side crown molding in place and mark the bottom edge where it meets the corner of the case. Cut at this mark with a compound bevel cut. If you use the table saw, set the miter gauge at 22½° and hold the molding at a 45° angle to the saw table as you cut. If you use a power miter saw, set the saw at 22½° and hold the molding so that it leans at a 45° angle against the back fence, upside down. Cut it a little long the first time, then cut the side pieces and check the way the 2 pieces meet before trimming each piece to its final length. The back ends of the side crown moldings should be cut square, flush with the back edge of the case. When all the crown molding pieces fit together nicely, glue and nail them to the case (but not to the top).

Draw a pencil line on the top along the outside edges of the crown molding; remove the top, trim it to the line, and permanently nail or screw it in place. Plane or sand it down where necessary so that it is perfectly flush with the crown molding. Cut the half-round moldings (N, O, and P) and glue and nail them so that they cover the edge of the top and the joint between the crown molding and the top. Thoroughly wipe away any excess glue with a damp rag; set the nails and putty the holes.

10. Attaching the base molding

Set the table-saw blade to 45° and rip the upper edge of a length of 3¼-inch-wide stock that is long enough to make the base moldings (Q, R, and S). Miter these pieces at 22½° where they meet (the cuts are not sprung as the crown molding cuts were). Glue and nail the base molding pieces flush with the bottom edge of the case.

11. Attaching the feet

Cut the 4 feet (T). Using the router with the quarter-rounding bit, round over all 4 edges on the ends that will make contact with the floor. This will help keep them from splintering if the piece is moved around. Glue and screw the feet in place—the back ones should be positioned flush with the rabbets on the side pieces, and the front ones directly against the inside of the face frame.

12. Making the door frames

The wood for the door stiles (U) should be chosen carefully for straightness and evenness of grain—any warp in these pieces can make it very difficult to hang the doors straight. Knotty wood should not be used. Cut the door rails (V) to length, using an end stop on the table saw or radial arm saw to be sure that the rails are all exactly the same length. Their ends must be perfectly square as well.

Clamp the door frames together as they will go, then make 2 marks across each joint where the dowel pins will go. Now, with the frames clamped together and laid out on the workbench, use the router with a chamfering bit to put a ¼-inch-wide chamfer around the inside edges of the frames; the chamfer will hold the panels. The router will leave the corners rounded, but they can be easily squared with a sharp chisel after assembly. Check the inside measurements of the door frames for the panel sizes before unclamping the frames.

Now drill the holes where marked for ⅜-inch by 2-inch dowel pins—12 in each door. Finally, cut ¼-inch by ¼-inch grooves in the door-frame pieces that will hold the panels, with either a dado cutter in the table saw or the router with a slotting cutter. The grooves on the rails can be cut from end to end; the stile grooves should stop 2½ inches from each end. Note that the center rail has grooves on both sides.

13. Installing the door panels

Select good, flat pieces of 1×12 for the panels (W and X) and cut them to the proper sizes. They should be ½ inch larger than the frame openings in both directions, to allow for some expansion. Put a 60- or 100-tooth carbide blade on the table saw, and set the blade angle for 13°. The blade should project 2 inches above the saw table. Test the cut on a scrap piece to be sure that the panel edge will fit in the grooves in the door frames. Make the angle cut as shown

in the detail (see page 52) all the way around one face of each panel. Reset the saw blade to 90°, so that it projects only ⅛ inch above the bed, then make the bead cut as shown on page 52. Sand carefully to remove saw marks without rounding, or "smudging," the bead. Dry-assemble the doors to check the fit of the panels; sand or recut them if they are too tight. Apply glue to the meeting surfaces and in the holes for the dowel pins, insert the dowel pins, and assemble the doors; clamp; thoroughly wipe away any excess glue with a damp rag, and check for flatness.

14. Edging the doors

When the glue on the doors is dry and the joints have been flattened and rough-sanded, use the router with the chamfering bit to cut a ¼-inch-wide chamfer around the outside edges of the doors—but not on the edges where the doors will meet. Next set the table saw to cut the ⅜-inch by ⅜-inch rabbet around the 3 outside edges on the back of each door. Again, the meeting edges of the doors should be left square. With glue and brads, apply a strip of flat molding called an astragal (Y) to the right-hand door so that it overlaps the left-hand door.

Sand the surfaces of the doors with 100-grit sandpaper to remove all work marks, then hand-sand all the edges to soften them.

15. Installing the adjustable shelves

Make as many adjustable shelves (AA) as you need by cutting pieces of veneered plywood to fit inside the case. Edge-band their front edges. Support the shelves with shelf clips (available at most hardware stores); drill holes for them with a ¼-inch bit and a homemade hole-drilling jig. Make the jig by drilling a straight line of ¼-inch holes at regular intervals down the center of a 28-inch 1×2 or plywood scrap (see page 56).

16. Hanging the doors

Use ⅜-inch offset cabinet hinges for hanging the doors. Adjust the hinges up or down until the doors meet properly. Install a clip catch to hold the left-hand door shut. Put a small lock with an old-fashioned key (available through woodworking or cabinet supply stores) on the right-hand door.

17. Attaching the back

Cut the back (Z) and nail it in place with small nails or brads every 6 inches around its edges. It is important that the case be on a flat surface and square when the back is applied, to avoid permanently twisting the case.

Completely sand the piece with fine sandpaper. Apply stain if desired, and use several thin coats of varnish to finish it, removing whatever hardware you can beforehand.

ARMOIRE/ENTERTAINMENT CENTER

This large armoire has concealed side compartments for tape and record storage, as well as two front compartments for a television, a VCR, and stereo equipment. The design has elements of primitive Gothic furniture but goes well in modern settings.

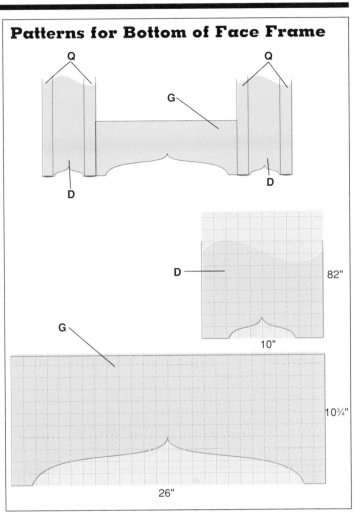

Patterns for Bottom of Face Frame

You'll need a fairly complete array of power tools for this large and complicated project: a table saw; a portable circular saw or a panel saw; a route; drill and doweling jig; and a saber saw (jigsaw). A power miter saw and a jointer would be helpful.

This project will consume three sheets of ½-inch birch plywood and 2 sheets of ¾-inch veneered plywood. Any solid wood and matching veneer can be used; birch and cherry go well together and are usually not too expensive. Use ½-inch birch plywood for the partitions (A) and back (C), to make the piece as light as possible without sacrificing strength.

1. Cutting the partitions

Cut the 2 partitions (A) from one sheet of ½-inch birch plywood. The scrap left over at the end of this sheet can later be used to make adjustable shelves (not shown). Make sure that the long edges of these pieces are very straight; use an electric hand planer to straighten your saw cuts if necessary. Then lay the partitions on a worktable with their inside faces up; mark the bottom of the lower dado 10 inches from the bottom edge, and the bottom of the upper dado 42⅛ inches from the bottom edge. Use a router with a ¾-inch straight cutting bit and a clamped-on guide to cut these dadoes ¼-inch deep across the full width of both pieces.

2. Attaching the center shelves

Cut the 2 center shelves (B). Lightly sand the shelves and the partitions, brush glue into the dadoes and onto the edges of the shelves, and clamp this center assembly together (see page 88). Thoroughly wipe away any excess glue with a damp rag. Check for squareness before setting the assembly aside to dry. If necessary, temporarily attach diagonal braces to keep the assembly square.

Hole-Drilling Jig for Adjustable Shelves

Stop made from closet pole dowel

Cabinet side, back, or front

2"

3/4"

3/4"

1/2"

1/4"

3. Cutting the back

Cut the back (C), being sure that the edges are straight. Make a hole-drilling jig like the one shown. In the outer portions of the back, where the side compartments will be, locate holes for shelf clips to support any adjustable shelves you may wish to install. Drill the holes between 10¾ inches and 42 inches above the floor, and between 43½ inches and 77 inches above the floor; use a ¼-inch bit. Drill similar hole arrangements into the sides of the central compartment, if extra shelves are desired. The 2 outer edges of the back must be edge-banded with veneer tape because the edges will show on the finished piece; see page 59. Set the back aside and allow the contact cement to dry for a day before trimming the tape.

4. Making the face frame

Cut the upright pieces (D), the top and bottom rails (E and G), and the middle rail (F), making sure that the ends of the rails are perfectly square in both directions, and that the rails are all the same length. The edges of the uprights must also be very straight and square. Expand the patterns for (D) and (G), transfer them, and cut the curved cutouts with a saber saw, using a fine-toothed blade; cut from the back. Sand the edges carefully. Lay the pieces out as they will go, and mark across the joints to position the holes for the dowel pins. Use a doweling jig to drill ⅜-inch holes for the 16 dowel pins (⅜ inch by 2 inch). Drill ¼-inch holes in the back of the uprights for adjustable shelves, using the hole-drilling jig that is illustrated; measure carefully so that the holes align with those you drilled into the back of the piece.

Materials List

Dimensions are finished size (in inches). Dimensions for shaped pieces are for stock from which piece is cut.

Part	Qty.	Description	Size/Material
A	2	Partitions	½ × 23½ × 82 birch plywood
B	2	Center shelves	¾ × 23½ × 26½ birch plywood
C	1	Back	½ × 46 × 82 birch plywood
D	2	Face-frame uprights	¾ × 10 × 82 veneered plywood
E	1	Face-frame top rail	¾ × 8½ × 26 veneered plywood
F	1	Face-frame middle rail	¾ × 2 × 26 solid cherry
G	1	Face-frame bottom rail	¾ × 10¾ × 26 veneered plywood
H	2	Top spacers	¾ × 5 × 23½ birch plywood
I	2	Fixed middle shelves	¾ × 8¼ × 23½ birch plywood
J	2	Fixed bottom shelves	¾ × 8¼ × 23 birch plywood
K	2	Bottom spacers	½ × 10 × 23½ birch plywood
L	2	Top moldings, side	¾ × 3½ × 25¾ cherry
M	1	Top molding, front	¾ × 3½ × 47¾ cherry
N	2	Top moldings, side	¾ × 3½ × 26½ cherry
O	1	Top molding, front	¾ × 3½ × 49¼ cherry
P	1	Top	½ × 25¾ × 47¾ birch plywood
Q	4	Fascia pieces	⅜ × 1¾ × 77 cherry
R	2	Side doors	¾ × 23¼ × 76½ veneered plywood
S	2	Front doors	¾ × 24½ × 28⅞ veneered plywood
T	4	Side moldings	¾ × 1 × 30⅜ cherry
U	4	Top and bottom moldings	¾ × 1 × 26 cherry
V	4	Adjustable shelves	½ × 8¼ × 23⅜ birch plywood

Hardware

3d, 4d, and 6d finishing nails
6 concealed hinges
¾" brads
4 touch-latch catches
4 butt hinges
Veneer tape
⅜" × 2" dowel pins
Shelf clips

Brush glue into the holes and onto the dowel pins and all the meeting edges, then insert the dowel pins; use bar clamps to bring all the pieces together. Be very careful to get the surfaces of the plywood pieces flush at the joints—since the cherry veneer is very

Exploded View

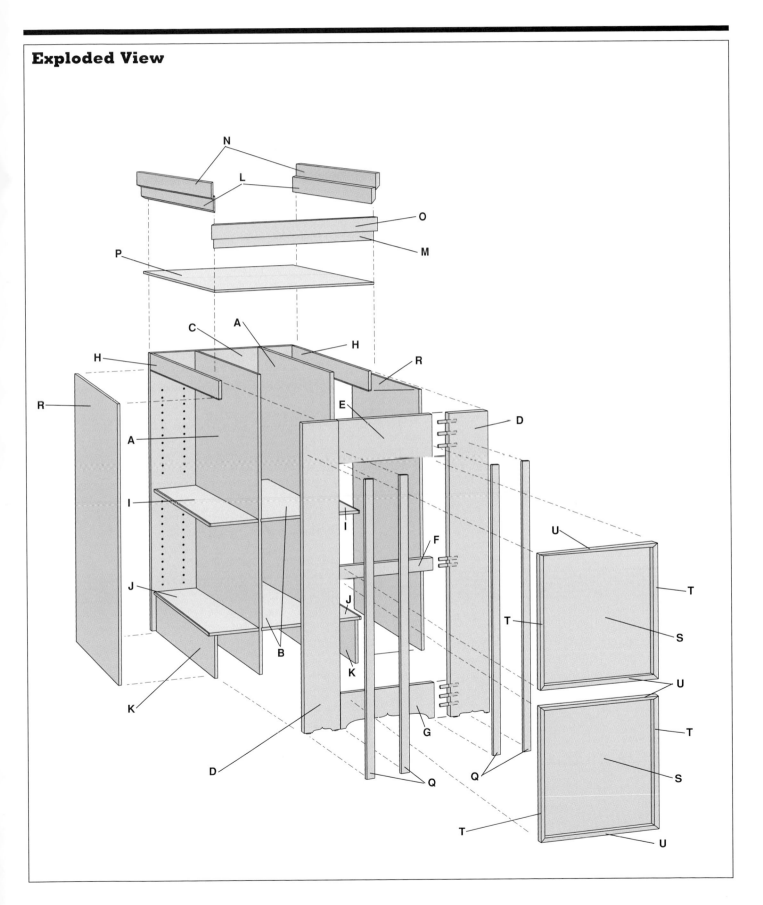

thin, you won't be able to sand these joints down flat later as you could with solid wood. Use a straightedge to be sure that the assembly is flat before setting it aside to dry. Thoroughly wipe away any excess glue with a damp rag.

Edge-band all exposed edges. You will not need to band the outside top and bottom edges. Let the contact cement dry for a day or so before trimming the veneer tape flush with the plywood.

5. Attaching the back and face frame

The edges where the shelves meet the partitions should all be flush and free of glue or other obstructions. Use a hand plane to smooth out any unevenness. Lay the partition/shelf assembly on the work surface with the front side up. Check to be sure that the tops of the center shelves will be flush with the tops of the rails and that the partitions will be flush with, or slightly back from, the inside edges of the uprights. Apply glue to the edges of the partitions and the center shelves, and use 6d finishing nails through the uprights (they'll be covered up later). Use bar clamps from front to back to hold (F) and (G) tightly to the shelves until the glue dries. Make sure that the partitions stay parallel to each other near the top where they are not held by a shelf.

Once the glue dries and the clamps can be removed, turn the assembly over and nail the back to it with 4d finishing nails (glue is optional). Again be sure that the partitions are parallel to each other and equidistant from the edges near the top where they are not held apart by a shelf.

6. Attaching the side shelves and spacers

Cut the fixed shelves (I and J) and the spacers (H and K). The ends of these pieces should be cut carefully so that they fit tightly between the front and back, but not so tightly as to force them away from the partitions. Completely sand and finish these pieces before they are put in place; edge-band the edges of (H), (I), and (J) that will be visible. Apply glue to the ends of these pieces, clamp them in place, and drive 3d or smaller finishing nails into them through the front (where trim will conceal them) and back to hold them in place. Install the bottom spacers in the same way. Attach them to the bottom shelves with small finishing nails.

7. Attaching the top moldings and top

The top-molding pieces (L, M, N, and O) are all of the same width—3½ inches. Start by cutting 2 pieces, each 9 feet long, then ripping a 45° bevel along one edge of each piece with a table saw. Miter the pieces to the proper lengths

with a miter box or power miter saw. The back ends of (L) and (N) are cut square, and fit flush with the back surface of the piece. Cut the miter cuts so that all the pieces are a little long at first, then clamp all 3 pieces of each layer in place and recut until the joints are just right. The thin edges of (L) should be flush with the bottom of the top spacers (H). Glue and nail the 2 (L) pieces in place, then mark a line 1 inch down from their top edges and align the second layer on it. After applying glue where the 2 layers meet, clamp the second layer in place and nail through the miter joints and along the angled edge with small finishing nails.

Cut the top (P) to fit as closely as possible to the inside edges of (N) and (O) on the front and on the sides, and flush with the back. Glue and nail the top to the top edge of the spacers, the back, and the face frame.

8. Attaching the front trim

Make the 4 vertical fascia pieces (Q). Set the table saw at a 22° angle and bevel the edges of the pieces. Use a hand plane or belt sander to refine the shape to a smooth arc, and use finish sanders to remove all work marks. Cut the top ends of all 4 fascia pieces at a 45° angle so that they fit tightly against the lower edge of (M). Attach them with glue and ¾-inch brads. Their edges should help cover the edges of the edge banding on the face-frame pieces.

9. Making the side doors

Cut the large side doors (R) to size and edge-band them. Use at least 3 concealed hinges for each door. A touch-latch mechanism (available at most hardware stores) acts as a catch for the doors, springing them open when pushed gently. This makes it unnecessary, to have handles on the doors, so the doors can appear to be just the sides of the cabinet.

10. Making the front doors

Cut the 2 front doors (S) 1½ inches smaller in both directions than the size of the openings, to allow for the edge moldings. Cut the molding pieces (T and U) to size, then round the outer edge with the router. Miter the ends and attach the strips to the edges of the doors with glue and 3d finishing nails. Mount the doors with either small butt hinges or concealed hinges; use touch-latch catches as with the side doors.

11. Finishing the piece

Set and putty all nails. Finish-sand the piece. Remove as much hardware as possible before applying an oil or varnish finish. Extra shelves (not shown) can be made for both the side and middle compartments from ¾-inch plywood; use veneer tape on all the visible edges.

SPORTS BOX

This design is actually taken from an Early American firewood box. Baseball bats, tennis rackets, and other long-handled equipment can go in the upper compartment, and gloves, balls, and so on can be kept in the drawer—or maybe you really do want to use it for firewood, in which case the lower compartment is just right for paper or kindling.

Tools required are a table saw or radial arm saw; a jointer; a table saw or router; a saber saw (jigsaw) or band saw; and a drill with a pilot-hole cutter and a plug cutter.

Walnut was used for this piece, but any hardwood would work. Softwoods, such as redwood, fir, or pine, would also work well. A plywood

version would be even easier to build, but the exposed edges would have to be veneered. If you use lighter-colored woods, you may want to apply a stain or paint.

1. Cutting the side and bottom panels

Except for the ¼-inch plywood drawer bottom, this project is

Edge Veneers

Veneer tape is available in many of the same materials from which plywood face veneers are made. This tape can be added to the exposed edges of plywood. The process of attaching the tape, called edge-banding, is easy. First make sure that the joints are flush and the edges are free of dried glue or other small imperfections. Then cut a strip of veneer tape to the exact length of each exposed plywood edge (don't trim the tape to the exact width; it should be wide enough to overlap both edges slightly). Where two edges intersect, cut the corners of the strips at 45° angles for a miter joint. Next brush two coats of contact cement onto the edges of the plywood and one even coat onto the underside of the veneer tape. Allow the ce-

ment to dry long enough to get tacky. Then apply the tape carefully. Once the cemented surfaces touch each other, the bond is complete; you can't reposition the tape without breaking the bond or damaging the tape. To ensure perfect alignment, place toothpicks across the plywood edges every 4 to 5 inches and set the veneer tape on them. Align the tape carefully. Then, starting at one end, pull the toothpicks out as you press the tape into place. Allow enough time (several hours) for the cement to set up, according to label directions. Trim the veneer tape flush with a razor blade or sharp knife and sand the edges of the tape flush with both faces of the plywood. Clean off excess cement with contact-cement solvent.

made entirely from ¾-inch solid lumber, such as 1✕4 or 1✕6. You may find you need to straighten and thickness-plane the lumber with a jointer and planer. Select enough 1✕6 lumber to make the sides (A) and the bottom (F), and crosscut the pieces to length. Use a jointer to straighten the edges. Lay the pieces out side by side (for edge-joining, see page 88). Use a square to mark across the edges for ⅜-inch by 2-inch dowel pins, 3 in each joint (be careful not to place them where they will be cut away later). Drill the holes, apply glue evenly to the meeting edges and dowel pins and in the holes, and insert the dowel pins. Thoroughly wipe away any excess glue with a damp rag. Use bar clamps (see

page 88) on alternating sides of the panel to press the joints together until the glue dries. Use a straightedge to be sure that the assemblies are flat.

2. Making the drawer-support frame

Cut the 4 pieces for the drawer-support frame (D and E) and join them with 2 dowel pins at each joint to form the frame. Check the assembly to be sure that it is flat and square, then set it aside to dry.

3. Cutting the front and back pieces

Cut the front board (C). Mill the back boards (B) with an overlapping V-groove pattern to allow expansion, using a jointer and a router or table saw (note that the back boards are 1 inch shorter than the front board). If you don't have the equipment or don't wish to take on this tedious job, you can buy ready-made V-groove lumber in softwoods, or cut the back from ½-inch or ¾-inch plywood.

4. Cutting the side panels

When the glue has dried on the sides and bottom, use a hand plane or belt sander to even up the edge joints. Now mark the sides for the curved cuts that form the legs, the straight cuts where the front board fits, and the curves on the top ends. Expand and transfer the pattern, or use a long, thin scrap with a nail through it for a compass (the center is 13 inches below the top along the back edge) to mark the curve for the top cut. Use a saber saw to make the curved cuts, and a circular saw or handsaw to make the straight cuts.

5. Cutting the side dadoes

The 2 dadoes for the bottom and the drawer-support frame are most easily cut using the router with a straight cutting bit and a clamp-on guide. The cutting-bit diameter should be the same as the thickness of (D) and (E)—¾ inch for plywood, 11/16 inch for some softwoods, and 13/16 inch for some hardwoods. Make the cuts ¼ inch deep. Stop the lower dado ¾ inch from the front edge. Cut a rabbet ¾ inch deep by ⅜ inch wide (when viewed from the back) into the back inside edges of the side pieces, using the table saw.

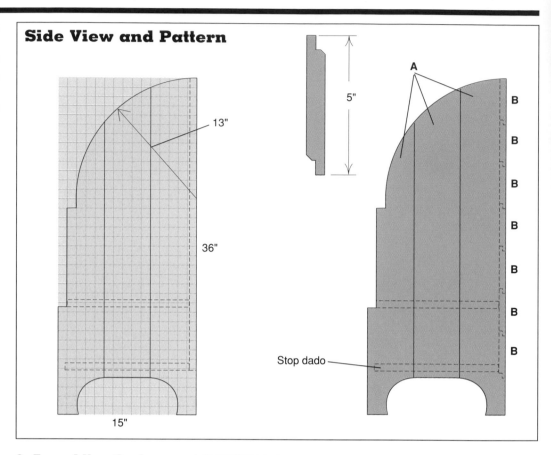

Side View and Pattern

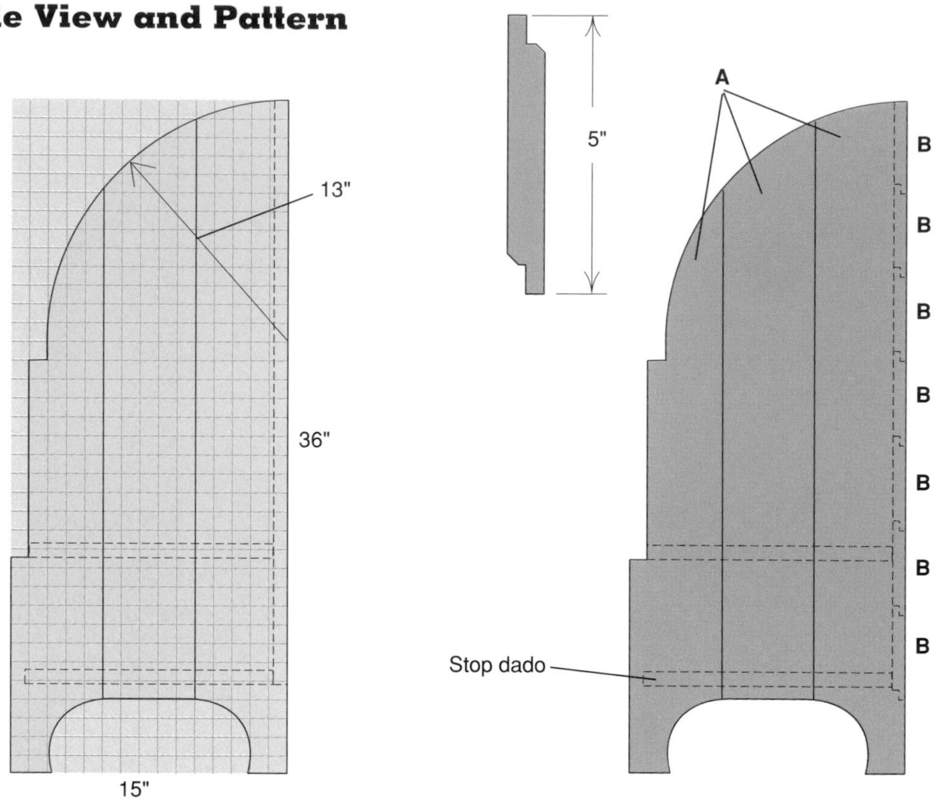
13"
36"
15"
5"
A
B
B
B
B
B
B
B
Stop dado

6. Assembling the frame

Dry-assemble the various pieces to be sure that everything fits, then apply glue in the 2 dadoes for the bottom, and on the ends of the bottom and the ends of the front piece (D) of the drawer-support frame. Use bar clamps—2 in front and 2 in back—to assemble these pieces. Check the assembly for squareness by measuring the diagonals of the opening, then clamp the front board in place. Counterbore pilot holes for screwing the front to the sides and the sides to the bottom. Unclamp the front board and apply glue where it will contact both the sides and the bottom before

Materials List

Dimensions are finished size (in inches). Dimensions for shaped pieces are for stock from which piece is cut.

Part	Qty.	Description	Size/Material
A	2	Sides	¾ X 15 X 36, made from 3 each ¾ X 5 X 36 boards
B	7	Back boards	¾ X 5½ X 35 hardwood
C	1	Front board	¾ X 11½ X 36 hardwood
D	2	Drawer supports	¾ X 2 X 35 hardwood
E	2	Drawer supports	¾ X 4 X 9¼ hardwood
F	1	Bottom	¾ X 14¼ X 35, made from 3 each ¾ X 4¾ X 35 boards
G	1	Drawer front	¾ X 5 15/16 X 34 7/16* hardwood
H	2	Drawer sides	¾ X 5 15/16 X 13½* hardwood
I	1	Drawer back	¾ X 5½ X 34 7/16* hardwood
J	1	Drawer bottom	¼ X 13½ X 33 7/16 plywood*

Hardware

1½" drywall screws
4d or 6d finishing nails
⅜" X 2" dowel pins
Drawer pulls
*Size of drawer pieces varies, depending on size of opening and type of drawer construction.

Exploded View

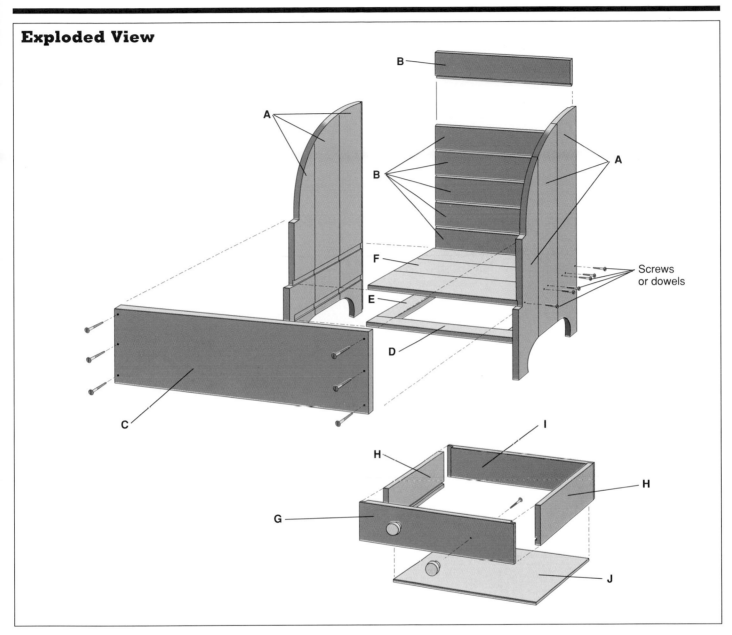

reclamping and inserting the screws. Cut plugs from the same type of wood (plug cutters should be used in a drill press) and glue the plugs into the counterbores. Thoroughly wipe away any excess glue with a damp rag.

7. Adding the back

Nail the back boards into place with 4d or 6d finishing nails. Use one nail at each end of each board—centered—to allow expansion of the boards. Rip the last board flush with the tops of the sides. A couple of finishing nails can also be driven through the lower edge of the front board and through one of the back boards into the bottom.

8. Making the drawer

Make the drawer using one of the drawer-construction methods presented in "Making Drawers" (see page 90) to fit in the 6-inch by 14¼-inch by 34½-inch space. A drawer of this size will work nicely without manufactured drawer slides. However, if you want to use them, either they will have to be bottom-mounted or you will need to adapt the drawer dimensions for side-mounted slides. Attach the drawer pulls.

9. Finishing the box

Sand the curved edges by hand until they are smooth, then use an orbital sander with 100-grit sandpaper to remove all work marks and to prepare the piece for finishing. An oil or light varnish finish will help protect the piece and bring out the natural beauty of the wood.

SHOP AND YARD PROJECTS

There's no need to limit your woodworking skills to furniture and indoor pieces. Put them to good use to make your shop more efficient and your yard more attractive. From utilitarian to whimsical, these six projects offer a wide range of woodworking challenges. You may want to build the router table and cabinet first. This project expands the capabilities of your router—for making intricate sliding dovetail joints, for instance—and enables you to build many of the more complex pieces in this book. You may also want to use up some scrap lumber and build a few whirligigs for your own pleasure and the amusement of others. The two designs in this chapter offer a starting point for you to try your own versions of this delightful folk craft.

The router is a versatile power tool that performs a variety of operations. With a straight bit, as shown here, it can cut grooves, dadoes, and rabbets. With a round-over bit, which has a pilot bearing built into it for guiding the tool in a straight line, you can use the router to shape the edges of boards into a rounded profile. Other profiles are possible with molding bits of various shapes and sizes.

ROUTER TABLE AND CABINET

The router is among the most versatile and powerful tools in a small woodworking shop. One of the best ways to use it is to mount it in a router table such as this one, designed to handle heavy-duty routers with large ½-inch arbor bits. Note that a clamp-on fence, not shown in the photograph, is included in this project.

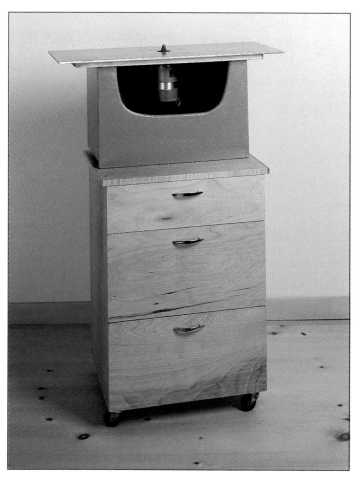

Tools required are a table saw or radial arm saw; a saber saw (jigsaw); a drill with a Phillips screwdriver bit, ³⁄₁₆-inch and ⅜-inch drill bits, and a counter-boring bit; and several short bar clamps. Once you've built the table and stand, you can mount your router in it and use it to finish this project.

One of the best materials for the case and table base is ¾-inch shop-grade birch plywood, but a better grade of Douglas fir plywood could also be used. The bare edges of the plywood may be banded with veneer tape (see page 59), if you like, or they may be left exposed. Quarter-inch aluminum sheet is the best material for the top, but steel will also work. You will need extra drawer material (½-inch plywood) for making trial sliding dovetail joints.

Materials List

Dimensions are finished size (in inches).

Part	Qty.	Description	Size/Material
A	2	Cabinet sides	¾ × 16 × 25 plywood
B	1	Cabinet bottom	¾ × 16 × 19 plywood
C	2	Cabinet stringers	¾ × 3½ × 18 hardwood
D	1	Cabinet back	¼ × 20 × 25 plywood
E	1	Cabinet top	¾ × 17 × 21½ plywood
F	1	Table back	¾ × 12 × 20 plywood
G	1	Table front	¾ × 12 ½ × 20 plywood
H	2	Table sides	¾ × 12 × 12 plywood
I	1	Subtop	¾ × 13½ × 23 plywood
J	1	Top	¼ × 16 × 26 aluminum sheet
K	1	Fence face board	¾ × 4 × 26 hardwood
L	1	Fence clamp board	¾ × 2 × 26 hardwood
M	2	Top drawer sides	½ × 2½ × 15½ plywood*
	2	Middle drawer sides	½ × 6 × 15½ plywood*
	2	Bottom drawer sides	½ × 11 × 15½ plywood*
N	1	Top drawer back	½ × 2 × 16⅜ plywood* **
	1	Middle drawer back	½ × 5½ × 16⅜ plywood* **
	1	Bottom drawer back	½ × 11 × 16⅜ plywood* **
O	1	Top drawer front	¾ × 4 × 19¾ plywood or hardwood*
	1	Middle drawer front	¾ × 7 × 19¾ plywood*
	1	Bottom drawer front	¾ × 12 × 19¾ plywood*
P	3	Drawer bottoms	¼ × 15 × 17 plywood*

Hardware

2 strap hinges (4")
4 casters
1¼" and 2" drywall screws
3 pairs full-extension drawer slides
Short length of chain
1" × #8 flat-head wood screws
3d finishing nails
1¼" × #10 flat-head wood screws

*Drawer dimensions are for sliding dovetail joinery. Check size of opening before cutting drawer pieces.
**Width of drawer allows ⁹⁄₁₆" clearance on each side for full-extension drawer slides. Check manufacturer's recommendation for your slides.

1. Making the cabinet case

Cut the cabinet sides (A), the bottom (B), the stringers (C), the back (D), and the top (E). Cut rabbets ¾ inch wide by ¼ inch deep (when viewed from the inside) on the bottom

Exploded View

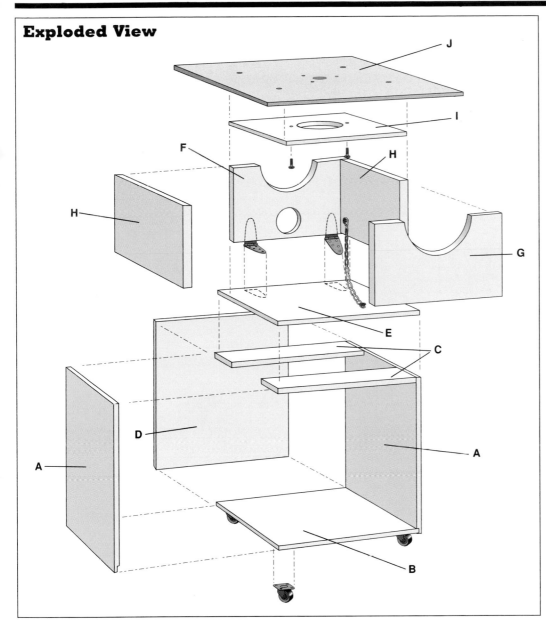

edges of the sides with 2 separate cuts on the table saw. Apply glue to the rabbets, the ends of the bottom, and the ends of the stringers; assemble, and use bar clamps (see page 88) to hold the pieces together. Drive 6d finishing nails through the sides into both the bottom and the stringers. Lay the cabinet face-down on the floor, check to be sure that it is square, and glue

and nail the back on with 3d finishing nails at 6-inch intervals. Finally, glue and screw the cabinet top down to the stringers and top edges of the sides with 1¼-inch drywall screws. The front and side edges of the top should overhang the cabinet by ¾ inch; the back edge is flush with the cabinet back.

2. Making the router table

Cut the back (F), the front (G), and the sides (H) of the router table. Make semicircular cutouts in the front and back pieces to be at least 6 inches deep and 12 inches across so that you can reach through them and comfortably operate the wrenches to change bits, and turn the router on and off or adjust its height. With a

router and ⅜-inch round-over bit, round over the cuts from both sides. Notice that the front is ½ inch taller than the sides and back. This will create a ½-inch space around 3 sides between the table and the cabinet top for easier dust removal. If you want to attach a dust collector to the router table, cut a round hole of the correct diameter out of the back piece, as close to the bottom as possible, and eliminate the ½-inch gap around the bottom by cutting all pieces the same height. To assemble the table, use 2-inch drywall screws and glue to attach the sides to the front and back, with all the top edges flush. Be sure that the assembly is square by measuring the 2 diagonals across the top. Thoroughly wipe away any excess glue with a damp rag before setting the table aside to dry.

3. Attaching the subtop

Cut the subtop (I). Find its center and mark out a circle slightly larger than your router base, just large enough for the base to fit through. Use a saber saw to cut out this circle. Before screwing the subtop down to the table, file or grind the tips off 2 screws, each 1¼ inch by #10. Bore 2 holes, ⅛ inch each, through the subtop 1 inch away from the circle cutout, on opposite sides. Turn the 2 blunted screws into these holes from the bottom side, so that they come up flush with the top. One of the problems with

Exploded View of Drawers

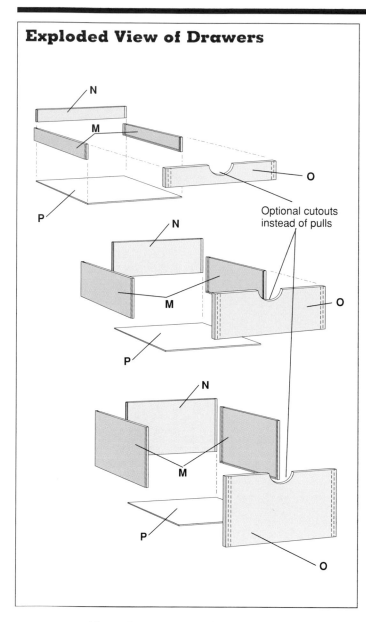

Optional cutouts instead of pulls

Clamp-On Fence

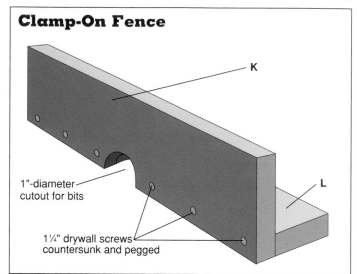

1"-diameter cutout for bits

1¼" drywall screws countersunk and pegged

Cutting Dovetail Tenon

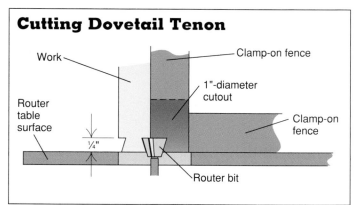

Work

Clamp-on fence

1"-diameter cutout

Router table surface

Clamp-on fence

¼"

Router bit

most router tables is their tendency to sag near the middle from the weight of the router. Once the tabletop has been screwed down to the subtop, these blunted screws can be used to adjust the top so that it is perfectly flat, or even bowed up just slightly near the middle. With these screws in place, glue and screw the subtop down to the table so that the back is flush and the sides and front overhang.

4. Attaching the top

The top (J) is made from a piece of ¼-inch sheet aluminum. Aluminum is ideal for this application because it is strong enough to hold the screws that attach the router base to it, it is easy to bore and cut, and it does not rust. Steel plate is less expensive, although more difficult to cut, and will also work. First find the center of the top and mark out a 1-inch-diameter circle

around it. Bore a ⅜-inch starter hole just inside this circle, then use the saber saw with a fine-toothed metal-cutting blade to cut out the circle.

Now unscrew the router base plate from the router base and center it over the hole in the top. Carefully mark the positions of the 3 or 4 screw holes that hold the base plate to the base by pushing a pencil tip through each hole and tracing the small circles onto the top. With a sharp punch and a hammer, punch a dent in the center of each hole so that the drill bit will not skid out of position when you begin drilling these holes. The hole sizes will vary with the make

of the router, but ³⁄₁₆ inch is typical. After boring these holes, use a beveled counterbore bit to cut the counterbores so that the heads of the machine screws that hold the router base to the top can be set slightly below the surface of the top.

Bore and counterbore 4 more screw holes, near the 4 corners of the top, so that the top can be screwed down to the subtop with 1-inch by #8 wood screws.

5. Attaching the table to the cabinet

Attach the table assembly to the cabinet top with strap hinges. Use the screws that are provided to attach the hinges as shown to the outside of the back and to the top of the cabinet top, so that there is a ½-inch space between the table and the cabinet top on all sides except the front (unless you're attaching a dust collector vacuum). Screw a short piece of chain to the inside of one side of the table and to the cabinet top so that the entire table assembly may be tilted back (the chain acts as a stop so that the table tilts only about 30°) for easier access.

6. Attaching the cabinet casters

You can buy, through woodworking tool suppliers, special heavy-duty casters with foot-operated locks that keep the casters from rolling while you are working. Or, if you don't want a mobile cabinet, you can create legs by simply screwing some square pieces of 2-inch by 2-inch by 1½-inch material to the cabinet.

7. Making the clamp-on fence

Use glue and nails or screws to join the 2 pieces of 1-by material (K and L) at right angles. Before joining these 2 pieces, be sure that the face board (K) is absolutely straight and square on the edge that will be joined to the clamp board (L) by running it on a jointer or carefully trimming it with a fine-toothed table-saw blade. Cut a 1-inch-diameter half circle into the edge of the face board, at midpoint, to provide clearance for the router bit when necessary.

8. Cutting the drawer pieces

Cut the drawer pieces (M, N, and O). The sides (M) and the backs (N) may be made from ½-inch-thick birch plywood; the fronts (O) may be made from the same material or from ¾-inch-thick solid wood. The drawer-construction method shown is called a sliding dovetail, which is made by using a ½-inch dovetailing bit on the router table. When using the table, hold work tightly against the fence, because the rotation of the router bit can force work away from it, and always feed work from right to left.

Begin by setting the router so that the router bit projects up through the table ¼ inch. Next clamp on the fence about an inch away from the bit and make a dovetail dado on a piece of scrap to use in setting the router bit for making the dovetail tenon. To make the tenon, move the fence over so that the bit projects out from it as shown (see detail). Cut both sides of another scrap piece and test the resulting tenon in the scrap dado. Adjust the fence in or out until the tenon fits snugly yet slides easily. Then cut dovetail tenons, using this pair of cuts, on the front edges of the drawer sides and on both ends of the drawer backs.

To make the dado cuts, set the router fence ¾ inch from the closest point of the bit. Cut a vertical dovetail dado on the inside face of each drawer side, ¾ inch from the back edge. Now reset the fence 1½ inches from the bit to make a stopped dado on each end of the inside faces of all the drawer fronts. (The distance from the fence must be changed if you're making the drawer fronts or backs a different width from that specified in the Materials List.) To do this, make 2 marks on the fence ½ inch away from the bit in each direction (1½ inches apart). Cut the dado by sliding the drawer front in from one direction until its trailing edge reaches the closer mark. Then back it out of the slot, turn the drawer front around, and slide it in from the other direction until the trailing edge reaches the other mark; then slide it back out as well. Make the dadoes for the top drawer front so that the sides will be flush with the *bottom* edge of the front. Make dadoes in the other 2 drawers so that the side pieces will be flush with the drawer fronts at the *top* edge.

9. Cutting grooves for the drawer bottoms

Proper organization will prevent mistakes in this step. Organize all the drawer sides in pairs, with the dovetail tenons facing forward and the dovetail dadoes facing each other. Change the router bit to a ¼-inch straight cutting bit and adjust the router so that the bit projects ¼ inch above the table. Set the fence ¼ inch away from the bit. Cut a groove ¼ inch wide by ¼ inch deep the full length of the inside face of each side piece, along the bottom edge. The pieces must be mirror images of each other, one right side and one left side, so pay attention while doing this. Cut grooves in the front pieces by plunge-routing. Lower the pieces slowly onto the bit, slide them forward, and lift them off so that the groove begins and ends at the dovetail dadoes and doesn't run beyond them to the edge.

10. Assembling the drawers

Cut the drawer bottoms (P). To assemble the drawers, brush glue into the bottoms of the dovetail dadoes in the front pieces and slide the sides into place so that the grooves align on all 3 pieces. If the tenons are so tight in the slots that you can't push them into place, use a bar clamp to move them together; avoid hitting or pounding them. Slide the backs into place in the same manner, so that the bottom edge of each is flush with the top of the groove. Thoroughly wipe away any excess glue with a damp rag. Slide the drawer bottoms in from the back. Be sure that the drawer is square when you set it aside to dry. Use diagonal braces to hold the drawers square if they won't stay that way by themselves.

11. Completing the project

After the glue has dried, nail the drawer bottoms to the edge of the back pieces with small brads. If desired, cover the exposed plywood edges of the drawers, cabinet, and table with veneer tape (see page 59) or small moldings. Sand the components and finish them with paint, stain, or clear sealer. Attach full-extension drawer slides to the drawers and cabinet sides (see pages 70 and 91); attach drawer pulls or cut out semicircles in the drawer fronts.

SHOP BENCH

This bench is designed to provide a large, clear work surface for laying out and gluing up pieces, plus ample storage for small tools. If you have room in your shop for only one bench, a vice and a series of holes for bench dogs could be added to this one. It can be free-standing or, if the top is offset 2 inches, installed with one end against a wall, as shown.

Tools required are a table saw or radial arm saw; a jointer; a router with ¼-inch and ½-inch straight cutting bits; a drill with a ⅜-inch bit, a doweling jig, a pilot-hole cutter, and a Phillips screwdriver bit; and at least half a dozen 48-inch bar clamps. A portable circular saw would also be handy for cutting down sheets of plywood to manageable sizes.

Kiln-dried hardwood such as fir or maple would be best for the work surface of the bench, but for economy you could use two layers of ¾-inch Douglas fir plywood, or even high-density particleboard. Shop-grade fir or birch plywood will be adequate for the case, and construction-grade lumber is acceptable for the stringers and end pieces. For the drawer sides and fronts, high-quality 7-ply ½-inch birch or mahogany plywood is recommended; ¼-inch plywood should be used for the drawer bottoms. Full-extension drawer slides make the drawers completely accessible.

1. Gluing the top

The top (A), which is 40 inches wide, is made from 8 pieces, each 7 feet long, of 2X6 Douglas fir, maple, or other very hard wood. The pieces should be checked carefully for straightness, and should be dry and well seasoned. Crosscut them to length, then run them on the jointer to straighten all the edges. Use 3 or 4 dowel pins (½ inch by 2 inch) per board to help strengthen the joints and align the boards. Start with 2 boards. Drill holes. Spread glue evenly on the meeting surfaces, on the dowel pins, and in all the holes; insert the dowel pins, and use clamps to bring the boards together (see page 88). Open the clamps, apply glue to the second set of meeting surfaces and holes, insert the dowel pins, and clamp the new board up to the first 2. When all the boards are assembled, alternate clamps on both faces of the top so that the pressure will be even. Wipe away as much squeezed-out glue as you can. Lay a straightedge across the assembly to be sure that it is flat. If the joints are slightly uneven, after the glue has dried, use a portable power planer or belt sander to smooth and flatten the surface.

2. Cutting the case pieces

Cut the bottom (B), the ends (C), the partition (D), and the 2 stringers (E). Cut a rabbet

Materials List

Dimensions are finished size (in inches).

Part	Qty.	Description	Size/Material
A	8	Work surface boards	1½ X 5 X 84 hardwood or Douglas fir
B	1	Case bottom piece	¾ X 36 X 79½ plywood
C	2	Case ends	¾ X 30¾ X 36 plywood
D	1	Case partition	¾ X 30¾ X 36 plywood
E	2	Stringers	1½ X 5½ X 78½ pine or Douglas fir
F	3	Short base pieces	1½ X 3½ X 29 pine or Douglas fir
G	2	Long base pieces	1½ X 3½ X 76 pine or Douglas fir***
H	2	Dividers	¾ X 30¾ X 38⅞ plywood
I	4	Top drawer sides*	½ X 5¼ X 23½ plywood
	4	Middle drawer sides*	½ X 9 X 23½ plywood
	4	Bottom drawer sides*	½ X 12 X 23½ plywood
J	2	Top drawer backs*	½ X 4¾ X 36 plywood**
	2	Middle drawer backs*	½ X 8½ X 36 plywood**
	2	Bottom drawer backs*	½ X 11½ X 36 plywood**
K	2	Top drawer fronts*	½ X 5¼ X 36 plywood**
	2	Middle drawer fronts*	½ X 9 X 36 plywood**
	2	Bottom drawer fronts*	½ X 12 X 36 plywood**
L	2	Top drawer faces*	¾ X 6 X 39 15/16 birch plywood or pine
	2	Middle drawer faces*	¾ X 9½ X 39 15/16 birch plywood or pine
	2	Bottom drawer faces*	¾ X 13 X 39 15/16 birch plywood or pine
M	6	Drawer bottoms*	¼ X 22¾ X 37 15/16 plywood
N	4	Sliding doors	½ X 20 X 29⅞ plywood
O	4	Door tracks	¾ X 2 X 38⅞ hardwood
P	****	Shelves	¾ X 9 X 38¾ plywood

Hardware

4d, 5d, 6d, and 8d finishing nails
1¼", 2", 2½", and 3" drywall screws
Full-extension drawer slides
Veneer tape
½" X 2" dowel pins
Shelf clips

*Drawer dimensions will vary depending on type of joinery and sliding hardware.
**Width allows 9/16" clearance on both sides of drawer for full-extension drawer slides. Check manufacturer's recommendation for your slides.
***If bench will be against wall, make these pieces 77½" long.
****Number of shelves depends on personal preference.

¾ inch wide by ¼ inch deep (when viewed from the inside) along the bottom edges of the ends where they meet the bottom. This can be done with 2 cuts on a table saw, but since this is a fairly large piece, it will be easier to cut the rabbet with a router and clamp-on straightedge. Cut 2-inch by 5½-inch notches in the upper corners of the partition to accommodate the stringers. You can also drill holes for adjustable shelf supports at this time, or wait until the bench is completed (see step 9).

3. Assembling the case

Apply glue to the edges of the bottom where it meets the ends; nail the ends to the bottom with 5d finishing nails. Lay out 2 guidelines across the bottom piece for the partition, ⅜ inch on either side of the midpoint and parallel to the ends. Apply glue to the bottom edge of the partition and use clamps to hold it in place between these lines while driving 2-inch drywall screws into it from below. Set the stringers in place on top of the partition and butting the ends; their tops should be flush with the tops of the ends. Screw the stringers to the ends using 2-inch drywall screws. Measure to be sure the partition is perfectly parallel to the end pieces before screwing down through the stringers with 3-inch drywall screws to hold it. Finally, draw vertical guidelines for the dividers (H) on the inside of each end piece and on both sides of the partition, 24 inches in from the edges on the side where the drawers will go. Cut the dividers (H) from ¾-inch

Exploded View

O

A

N

N

E

C

C

H

H

B

D

G

F

F

F

G

Drawer

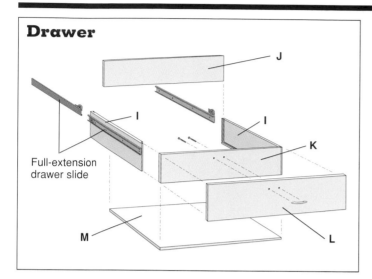

J

I

I

K

Full-extension drawer slide

M

L

plywood and slide them into place so that the sides facing the drawers are aligned along the guidelines. Hold the dividers in place with glue along the bottoms and 6d finishing nails along the ends. When the case has been completely assembled, cover the plywood edges with veneer tape (see page 59).

4. Attaching the base

Cut the base pieces (F and G) and nail or screw them together as shown. Center the base under the bench, or, if one end of the bench will be against a wall, make the base flush with that end. Drive 8d finishing nails down through the bottom of the case to attach it to the base.

5. Attaching the top

Position the top with 2 inches overhanging each end, or, if the bench will be against a wall, flush with that end. Drill pilot holes up through the stringers, and drive 2½-inch drywall screws up through the holes into the top to secure it.

6. Building the drawers

The drawers are designed to be mounted on full-extension drawer slides so that they can be pulled out all the way.

To build the first drawer, cut the sides (I), the front (K), and the back (J) pieces to size. The height depends on whether you start with a top, middle, or bottom drawer, but in each case the height of the drawer back is ½ inch less than that of the front. This is to allow the bottom to be slid into its slot from the back. Cut a rabbet ½ inch wide by ¼ inch deep (when viewed from the inside) along the front edge of each side for the drawer front, and a dado of the same size ½ inch in from the back of each side to hold the drawer back. This is best done with a ½-inch straight cutting bit on a router table. For the bottom (M), cut a ¼-inch by ¼-inch groove ¼ inch above the bottom edges of the 2 sides and the front. Since the bottom groove runs with the grain, this cut can be made with either the router or a dado cutter in the table saw.

Apply glue in the dadoes and the rabbets in the drawer sides. Thoroughly wipe away any excess glue with a damp rag. Position the drawer front in the rabbets and fit the back into the dadoes. Use short bar clamps to hold the pieces together, making sure that the grooves for the bottom are lined up precisely where the front meets the sides, and that the lower edge of the back piece is aligned with the top of the grooves. Nail the sides to the front and back, using 4d finishing nails. Next cut the bottom to size and slide it into the grooves from the back. Check the drawer for squareness, then nail the bottom to the lower edge of the back piece and let the drawer dry. Repeat for the other 5 drawers.

7. Installing the drawers

To mount the drawer slides on the partition and ends of the case, use a framing square to draw lines at right angles to the edges of these pieces 1 inch below where the top of each drawer will be. The front ends of the drawer slides should be flush with the front edges of the case. Mount the corresponding slide parts on the drawers themselves, 1 inch below the top. Install all the drawers in the case. Adjust the drawers carefully so that there is approximately ½-inch clearance above and below each of them.

8. Attaching the drawer faces

Cut the drawer faces (L). Drive 2 drywall screws (1¼ inch) through the front of each drawer from the inside so

that their tips just project through the front of the drawer. Apply glue to the inside of each drawer face and position it carefully on the drawer front so that it overlaps the side by ¾ inch and the partition (D) by ⁵⁄₁₆ inch. When the drawer face is properly lined up, press it against the protruding screws, pull out the drawer, and clamp the drawer face in place with C-clamps. Drive the screws all the way in.

9. Attaching the sliding doors

Cut the sliding door (N). Drill a 1-inch finger hole near the center of one edge (or the top, if you prefer) of each door, and use the router with a ¼-inch quarter-rounding bit to round all the edges.

Make the door tracks (O) from a hardwood such as maple. Cut 2 grooves ⁹⁄₁₆ inch wide and ¼ inch apart on one long face of each track, ⅝ inch deep for the upper tracks and ¼ inch deep for the lower tracks. Glue and nail the tracks in place so that they are flush with the outer edges of the case. To install the doors, slide them up as far as they will go into the upper track, then drop them into place in the lower track.

Use a ¼-inch drill bit and jig like the one shown on page 56, with a depth stop, to drill holes for shelf clips to support adjustable shelves inside the compartments behind the sliding doors. Make as many shelves (P) as you will need. Finish the case as desired.

This arched-top rose arbor is designed to disappear under a canopy of foliage and blossoms. The gate is a simple one, enhanced by the nicely shaped pickets and the rising line of their tops. Plant a red rose on one side and a yellow one on the other, water regularly, and let the passing seasons embellish your handiwork.

Arch Patterns

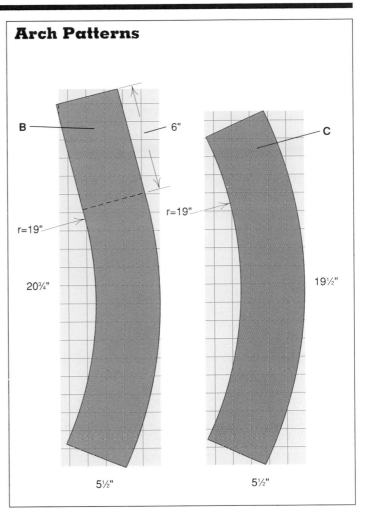

Tools required are a portable circular saw or saber saw (jigsaw); a drill and 5/16-inch and 1/8-inch bits; a short level; a posthole digger; a shovel; and a wheelbarrow. A band saw and a few C-clamps will be helpful. Hand tools, including a hammer, a chisel, and measuring tools, will also be needed.

Construction-grade lumber can be used for all the parts of this project, but be sure the wood is fairly straight and free of large knots and cracks. For the 2×6 arch pieces, choose flat-grain lumber (wavy pattern), not vertical grain (straight, parallel lines). The posts should be made from redwood, cedar, or pressure-treated lumber, to resist rotting caused by contact with the ground.

1. Cutting the posts

The 2 posts (A) are intended to be set into the ground 2 feet and project 6½ feet above the ground. Cut the posts with their tops square, and be sure that both posts are exactly the same length. Draw lines across the posts 6 inches from the top and use a square to extend these lines all the way around both posts. On any face of the posts, draw 2 lines parallel to the sides, 1 inch from each edge, from the horizontal lines up the 6 inches to the end of the posts. Extend the lines over the top and down the opposite face to the horizontal lines. These lines are for cut-

ting notches on both sides of both posts to accommodate the bases of the arch pieces. Set a portable circular saw so that the blade is cutting just 1 inch deep, and carefully cut on the horizontal lines. Repeat at 1-inch intervals up the 6 inches to the end of each post. Use a hammer and chisel to chip away the waste on both sides of the posts until the tenon that remains on the end of each post is smooth and flat.

2. Digging the postholes

The posts should be set so that their inside edges are 38 inches apart, so mark their centers 41½ inches apart on the ground. To keep the posts in line with the fence, stretch a string line in both directions along several fence posts. Dig the postholes 24 inches deep and 9 inches or more across. Lay both posts on the ground, at right angles to the gate line and parallel to each other, with the broad side of the tenons facing up. Measure up about 30 inches from the bottom of each post and draw a line across each post at this point. Tack a 45-inch-long scrap of 1-by material across both posts so that its top edge is on the lines and the inside edges of the posts are 38 inches apart.

3. Setting the posts

With a helper, set the posts into the holes simultaneously. Put a level on the 1-by scrap and raise one post or the other until it reads level. Hold the post in position and shovel a little bit of gravel under it. Check the level, then shovel gravel around the bottom of both posts. (The gravel prevents the concrete from encasing the ends of the posts, which might form a pocket that collects moisture, causing the posts to rot faster.) When the posts are at the same level, tack diagonal braces to them as needed to hold them plumb. Check that they are 38 inches apart at the top as well as at the bottom. Now mix concrete in a wheelbarrow, one bag at a time, and work it down into the holes until it comes up to just above ground level. Finish the top of the concrete so that it slants away from the posts all the way around, and check again to be sure that the posts are plumb and parallel. Let

Picket End Pattern

2½"

the concrete cure for at least 24 hours.

4. Cutting the arch pieces

Expand the patterns for the arch base pieces (B) and the upper arch pieces (C), transfer them to 2×6 material, and cut 4 of each piece. Cut out a ½-inch-deep by 6-inch-long notch on the inside face of each arch base.

Lay out the 4 pieces for one layer of the arch on ½-inch-thick exterior-grade plywood; trace the outlines of the arch on the plywood to create the filler piece (D), which goes between the 2 outer layers of the arch. Cut this piece with a saber saw. (If you don't have a big enough piece of plywood, you can cut the filler piece in sections, as long as the breaks are as far away as possible from the joints in the outer layers.)

5. Assembling the arch

Dry-assemble the 3 layers of the arch. Measure across the base pieces to be sure that they will land properly on the ends

Materials List

Dimensions are finished size (in inches). Dimensions for shaped pieces are for stock from which piece is cut.

Part	Qty.	Description	Size/Material
A	2	Posts	3½ × 3½ × 102 heart redwood or pressure-treated lumber
B	4	Arch base pieces	1½ × 5½ × 20¾ heart redwood or pressure-treated lumber
C	4	Upper arch pieces	1½ × 5½ × 19½ heart redwood or pressure-treated lumber
D	1	Filler piece	½ × 22½ × 45 exterior plywood
E	18	Plant-support pieces	¾ × 1½ × 14 heart redwood
F	2	Gate-frame stiles	1½ × 3½ × 27 heart redwood or pressure-treated lumber
G	2	Gate-frame rails	1½ × 3½ × 33 heart redwood or pressure-treated lumber
H	1	Gate-frame brace	1½ × 3½ × 40 heart redwood or pressure-treated lumber
I	1	Picket	¾ × 2½ × 36 heart redwood
	2	Pickets	¾ × 2½ × 34 heart redwood
	2	Pickets	¾ × 2½ × 33 heart redwood
	2	Pickets	¾ × 2½ × 32 heart redwood
	2	Pickets	¾ × 2½ × 31 heart redwood

Hardware

1 pair 6" screw-hook-and-strap (pivot) gate hinges
1 gate latch
6d galvanized finishing nails
6d galvanized box nails
16d galvanized box nails or twist nails
Construction adhesive (exterior)
Concrete mix, as needed

of the post. Trim or shim as needed. Apply several beads of exterior construction adhesive to the inside surfaces of the outer layers of the arch; use C-clamps (see page 88) to hold them in place on the filler layer while you drive 6d galvanized finishing nails through from both sides. Apply exterior construction adhesive to the tenons on the ends of the posts, slip the arch over the tenons, and drive 6d galvanized finishing nails

through from both sides to hold the arch to the tenons.

6. Attaching the plant supports

Cut the 1×2 plant-support pieces (E) to length, then mark each one 5¼ inches from one end. Starting at the joints between the arch and the posts and working in both directions, use a square to draw marks across the outsides of the posts and arch at 11-inch intervals. Position the plant-

Exploded View

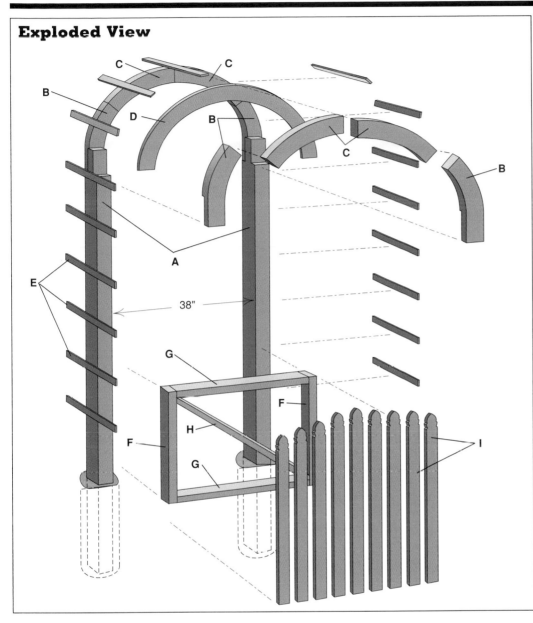

38"

support pieces with their top edges on the marks on the posts and the 5¼-inch marks on the edge of the posts. Nail each piece with 2 galvanized box nails (6d).

7. Building the gate frame

Cut the gate-frame stiles and rails (F and G). Predrill nail holes in the ends of the stiles with an ⅛-inch bit and nail the frame together with 16d galvanized box nails or twist nails. Cut the brace (H). Hold it in place on the frame (be sure that the frame is square), with one end at the lower hinge corner. Mark where it intersects each corner. Use a square to extend the cutting lines across the flat sides of the piece, then use either the circular saw or a handsaw to make the 2 cuts at each end.

Predrill nail holes through both the stiles and rails and nail the brace into place.

8. Attaching the hinges

Depending on which way you want the gate to swing, the hinges will be attached to the front or back side of the frame. Predrill bolt holes into the frame with a ⁵⁄₁₆-inch drill bit and bolt the straps to the gate. Hold or block the gate in position (at least 3 inches above

ground level) on the post to which it will be attached, and mark the centers of the holes for the hinge pivots about ¼ inch below the bottoms of the straps. Predrill these holes, then use a wrench or short length of pipe to screw the pivots into place. By turning one or the other pivot in or out a turn at a time, you can adjust the hang of the gate so that it is square to the posts.

9. Attaching the pickets

Cut the pickets (I) to length. Expand the pattern for the picket ends to full size, then transfer it to one picket and use the saber saw to cut it out. Use this piece to mark the rest of the pieces, then cut them out. Lift the gate frame off the posts and lay it on a flat work surface. Nail the 2 shortest pickets flush with the edges of the frame with 6d galvanized finishing nails. Their bottoms should extend about 1 inch below the bottom rail of the frame. Leaving about 1⅝ inches between pickets, lay them all out with their bottom ends even. Adjust the spacing so that it's even, then nail the pickets in place with 6d galvanized box nails. (You may have to cut notches across the backs of one or two pickets at one end to recess the hinge straps. Do this with multiple cuts of the circular saw set to cut ¼ inch deep.) Nail the pickets to the brace as well as the rails.

Hang the gate; screw a gate latch to the post opposite the hinges, and to the gate. Your gate and arbor are now ready to be primed and painted, or you can leave them natural.

VICTORIAN GATE

This formal Victorian gate will add a touch of elegance to any garden, and it is easier than it looks to build. The loose-tenon joinery that connects the rails to the stiles makes for very strong construction.

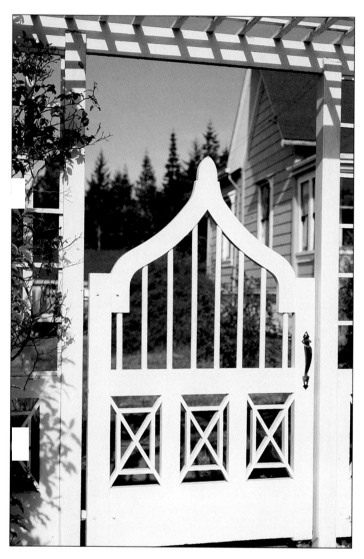

Materials List

Dimensions are finished size (in inches), except where noted. Dimensions for shaped pieces are for stock from which pieces are cut.

Part	Qty.	Description	Size/Material
A	2	Stiles	1½ × 4½ × 48 kiln-dried redwood
B	1	Middle rail	1½ × 4½ × 34½ kiln-dried redwood
C	1	Bottom rail	1½ × 10 × 34½ kiln-dried redwood
D	2	Upper pieces cut from	1½ × 8½ × 36 kiln-dried redwood
E	8	Upright dowels cut from	1" × 16' birch dowel
F	2	Frame uprights	1½ × 4½ × 16 kiln-dried redwood
G	6	X pieces	¾ × 1½ × 20 kiln-dried redwood
H	6	Upright panel pieces	¾ × 1½ × 10 kiln-dried redwood
I	6	Horizontal panel pieces	¾ × 1½ × 7 kiln-dried redwood

Hardware

½" × 3" dowel pins
4d galvanized finishing nails
1 pair 6" screw-hook-and-strap (pivot) gate hinges
1 gate latch

Tools required are a table saw or radial arm saw (or a portable circular saw with a cross-cutting guide); a saber saw (jigsaw); a miter box or power miter saw; a portable electric drill with a 1-inch spade bit; either a plunge router with a long straight cutting bit, or a ½-inch spade bit and chisels; and a sharp hand plane.

Kiln-dried redwood is a good, easy-to-work-with wood for this gate, but a stain-blocking primer paint should be used to keep the tannin in redwood from bleeding through the paint. Fir, pine, and other softwoods would also work well, if sealed and painted. If you use pressure-treated lumber, choose kiln-dried-after-treatment (KDAT). The drying process makes the lumber stable, so it won't shrink or warp. Keep in mind that the preservative does not penetrate completely through the lumber, so cutting and milling it reduces its resistance to rotting. It should be sealed and painted, as with other nondurable species.

Dimensions are for a gate 43 inches wide, but you can adapt them to other widths. The ideal size is 36 to 48 inches wide.

1. Cutting the frame pieces

Cut the stiles (A) and the rails (B and C). Expand the patterns for the 2 upper pieces (D) and transfer them to 2 lengths of 2×10, each 36 inches long. These pieces should be cut with a band saw if one is available; if not, use a saber saw. After cutting all the frame pieces, lay them out and check to be sure that the upper pieces fit nicely where they meet the stiles and each other. Use a hand plane, or recut if necessary, to flatten these areas so that the joints will be tight.

Exploded View

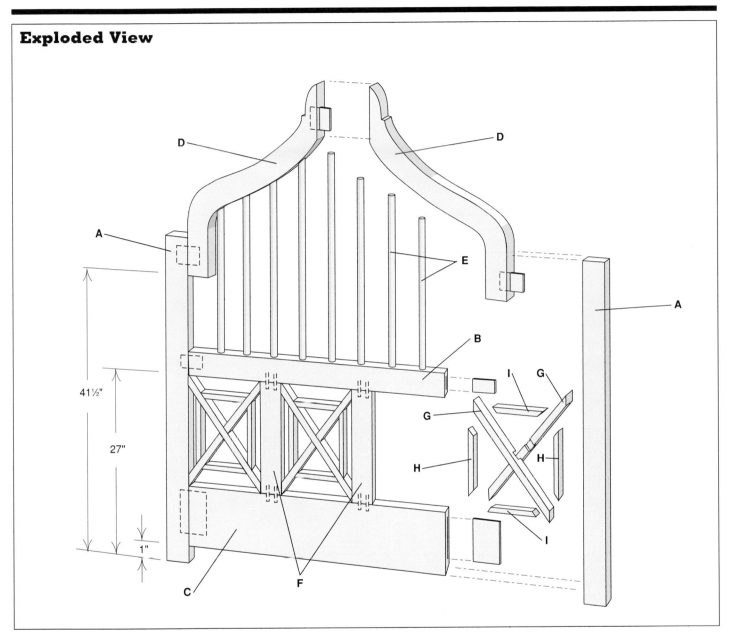

Labels: D, D, A, E, B, I, G, G, H, H, I, A, C, F

Dimensions: 41½", 27", 1"

2. Cutting the mortises

Lay the stiles on a workbench with their inner edges up; use a square to mark across them at 2 inches, 10 inches, 28 inches, 30½ inches, 42½ inches, and 47 inches from the bottom. These marks indicate the tops and bottoms of the 3 mortises that will be cut on both stiles. For the corresponding mortises, measure in 1 inch from the top and bottom of each rail and

from the bottom edge of each upper piece. For the mortises where the upper pieces meet, start at the bottom edge of the flat area where the 2 pieces meet and measure up 1 inch and 5 inches.

If you plan to use a plunge router to cut these mortises, you will need a 3-inch-long by ½-inch-diameter straight cutting bit and a fence attachment

for the router. Set the fence so that the cut will be as close to the middle of the edge of the stile as possible, and plunge the bit in about ½ inch for each pass. Make the cut in the direction that keeps the fence tightly against the stile, then pull out the bit, move the router back to the other end, and plunge the bit in ½ inch for another pass. Cut the mortises 2½ inches deep.

Optional Method You can also cut the mortises with just a drill and hand chisels. For this method, you will have to use a try square or marking gauge to mark lines ½ inch apart, parallel to the edges of the stiles and rails between the cross marks (see page 76). Use a ½-inch bit to drill out as much of the waste as possible, then use chisels to clean and square the mortises.

Cutting Mortises With a Drill and Chisel

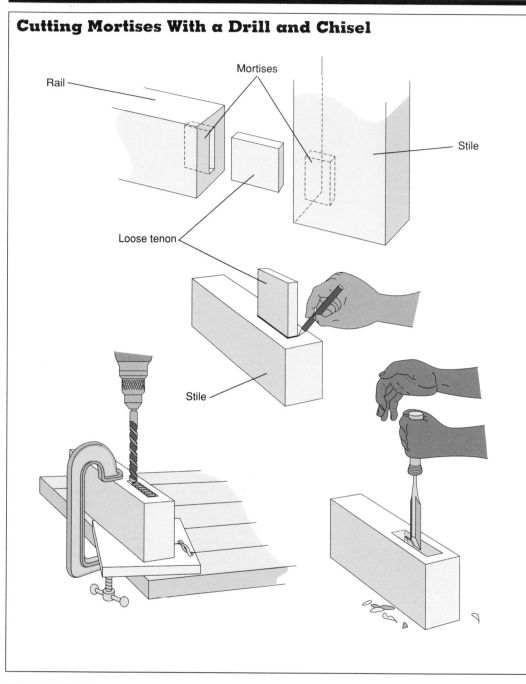

Rail

Mortises

Stile

Loose tenon

Stile

Upper Piece Pattern

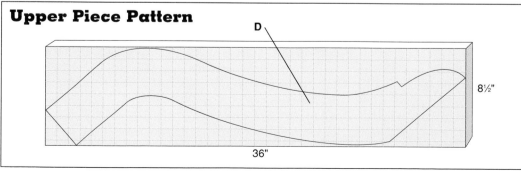

D

8½"

36"

3. Making the loose tenons

Plane or saw down to ½-inch thickness enough 1-by stock to make 7 loose tenons. Check the depth of your mortises, then cut the loose tenons to length so that they are a little shorter than the combined depth of the 2 mortises at each joint.

4. Cutting the frame uprights

Dry-assemble the stiles and the rails; check the distance between the 2 rails before cutting the 2 frame uprights (F) to length. Lay the uprights in place, positioning them so that the 3 panel spaces are of equal width; then mark across the joints between the rails and the uprights to position the dowel pins that will hold the uprights in place. Use a doweling jig and a ½-inch bit to drill the holes for the ½-inch by 3-inch dowel pins.

5. Assembling the frame

Use a waterproof urea-formaldehyde resin or resorcinol glue to assemble the stiles, the rails, and the uprights. (The upper pieces will be added later after the upright dowels have been prepared.) Spread glue in all the mortises and dowel-pin holes, on all the loose tenons and dowel pins, and on all the meeting surfaces. Insert the dowel pins and assemble the rails and uprights first, then insert the loose tenons in the mortises and fit the stiles on. Use bar clamps applied on alternate sides of the assembly to bring the joints tightly together (see page 88). Use a straightedge to be sure that the assembly is flat, and thoroughly wipe away any excess glue with a damp rag. After the glue has dried, plane or sand the joints flush where necessary.

6. Drilling holes for the upright dowels

Lay out the centers for the upright dowels (E) on the top of the middle rail by marking a centerline down the length of this surface, measuring in 1¾ inches from each stile for the first 2 dowels, then evenly spacing the remaining dowels 4¾ inches apart between the first 2 dowels. Set the 2 upper pieces in place, and transfer the center marks from the middle rail up to them by measuring the distances from one stile. Lay a straightedge across the middle rail and upper pieces to connect each pair of centers, then mark guide lines across the upper pieces. With a drill and 1-inch-spade bit, drill all the holes in the bottom faces of the upper pieces and in the middle rail to a depth of about 1 inch.

7. Completing the upright dowel assembly

Figure the lengths of the upright dowels by laying the upper pieces (D) in place again and measuring from hole to hole, then adding 1¾ inches (the combined depth of the holes less ¼ inch). Check to be sure that the dowels fit easily into the holes—you may need to sand or rasp the ends down a little if they fit too tightly. When all is ready, spread glue in the mortises and dowel holes, and on the meeting surfaces of the upper parts. Insert the loose tenons in the stiles first, then work

the dowels and upper pieces into place. Use bar clamps to tighten the joints at the stiles, and a couple of galvanized screws if necessary to bring the 2 upper pieces together in the middle. After the glue has dried, plane or sand the joints flush where necessary.

8. Installing the crosspieces

Rip about 20 feet of 1½-inch by ¾-inch stock for the 3 filler panels in the lower part of the gate. Begin by making the X pieces (G) for all 3 panels. Lay one piece diagonally across an open panel space from corner to corner. Mark the angles where the piece meets the framework; cut with a hand-saw or, if the angles are less than 45°, with a power miter saw. Repeat to make all 6 pieces, set them in place in the panel spaces, and mark where they meet for the half-lap cuts. Make these cuts on all 6 pieces with a handsaw to a depth of exactly ¾ inch, so that the pieces interlock and fit nicely in the panels. Glue the lap joints, then toenail the pieces in place with 2 galvanized finishing nails (4d) at each end.

9. Completing the filler panels

The 6 upright panel pieces (H) are approximately 10 inches long from point to point and are cut at 32° angles on their ends (lengths and angles may vary; take measurements to position the pieces as shown in the photograph, being sure that the outer edges align with one another). Cut the pieces and nail them in place so that they are parallel to the stiles. The horizontal panel pieces (I) are

about 7 inches long and are cut at 58° angles on their ends. Nail them in place so that they are parallel to the rails.

To finish the gate, putty all nail holes, sand, and apply one or more coats of exterior-

grade primer before a final coat of white enamel. Hang the gate with screw-hook-and-strap hinges or other heavy-duty gate hinges, then install the latch and strike plate.

Finishes for Outdoor Projects

There are 4 types of finishes intended to protect wood from weathering, each with advantages and disadvantages.

Wood Preservative

The principal ingredient of most wood preservatives is copper naphthenate, an environmentally approved chemical that turns the wood a deep greenish color, which eventually fades. Preservatives soak into the wood, helping it resist decay and insects. They are not water resistant and offer no protection from moisture. Preservative-treated wood can be stained, painted, sealed, or allowed to weather.

Sealer

Also called a water repellant, a sealer reduces warping, splitting, shrinkage, and swelling of the wood by forming a protective barrier against moisture. It is clear, but may be added to oil-based stains or paints. Some sealers contain fungicides and mildewcides; some have ultraviolet-light inhibitors, absorbers, or blockers. Both oil-based and water-based stains and paints may be applied over sealers, but sealers cannot be applied successfully over stained or painted wood.

Stain

Both semitransparent and solid stains protect the wood and add color. Some are oil-based, some water-based. Some have a sealer or preservative added. Semitransparent, or light-bodied, stains contain only a small amount of pigment and allow the grain pattern, texture, and some of the color of the wood to show through. Solid, or full-bodied, stains contain enough pigment to hide flaws, knots, grain pattern, and the original color of the wood; they act and look like paint, but without a glossy surface. Both types of stain should be renewed every year.

Paint

Besides offering a wide choice of colors, paint protects wood from ultraviolet-ray damage and allows you to hide cracks, joints, and flaws by filling them before painting. Exterior paint can be oil-based or water-based; choose a non-chalking type. For best results, apply a coat of sealer, then sand lightly before applying the primer and again before the finish coat of paint. Be sure to use a stain-blocking primer with redwood and other woods with dark tannins that might otherwise leach through the paint.

WHIRLIGIGS

Here are a couple of amusing ornaments for your garden or lawn. If you don't want to copy these designs, it's easy to come up with unique ones of your own. Just follow the basic format described in the instructions below and be creative.

One of the fun things about building these wind-powered ornaments is that most of the work can be done by hand. Check with your local hobby stores for materials that are already cut to convenient sizes and thicknesses if you don't want to use power tools to cut them down from thicker stock. A coping saw and a fine-toothed handsaw can do virtually all the cutting; a scroll saw would do the work more quickly. A drill with a selection of small bits, paints, brushes, and measuring and marking tools will also be needed.

Swimmer

Eighth-inch and ¼-inch-thick Finnish or Baltic birch plywood can usually be purchased at hobby stores, but if you can't find that, you can use ⅛-inch and ¼-inch mahogany plywood, which is made for door skins and is available in small sheets through most home centers. Both types of plywood are usually made with exterior-grade glues. When assembling the parts, be sure to use a waterproof glue such as a quick-drying epoxy or urea-formaldehyde resin glue.

1. Cutting the body

Expand the pattern for the swimmer's body (A) and transfer it to ¼-inch exterior-

grade plywood. Use a coping saw or saber saw with a narrow blade to cut out the pattern, then lightly sand the edges of the piece to smooth them. Paint the entire figure with primer. Use a pencil to draw the design on the figure, then use small brushes and weatherproof acrylic or exterior-grade paints to paint the body. Set it aside to dry, being careful not to smear it.

2. Making the arm-hub blocks

Cut the 2 arm-hub blocks (B). On one block, draw a diagonal line across one end. Then turn the block over and draw a

diagonal line across the other end, so that the 2 lines would form an X if you could see them both at once. Repeat on the other block. Put one of the blocks in a vise, with one end facing straight up, and use a fine-toothed handsaw (you may want to start the cut with a hacksaw) to cut a slot ¾ inch deep on the line. Widen this cut with a larger saw, a file, or

sandpaper until the ⅛-inch-thick stock that the arms will be made from can be slipped into it. Make the 3 other cuts the same way.

3. Making the arms

Expand the pattern for the arms (C) and transfer it to a piece of ⅛-inch exterior-grade plywood. Cut out 4 arms, apply a few drops of glue to

Materials List, Swimmer

Dimensions are finished size (in inches). Dimensions for curved pieces are for stock from which pieces are cut.

Part	Qty.	Description	Size/Material
A	1	Swimmer's body	¼ × 3 × 12 exterior plywood
B	2	Arm-hub blocks	½ × ½ × 2 pine
C	4	Swimmer's arms	⅛ × 1 × 3 exterior plywood
D	1	Pivot pin	⅛-diameter × 2 brass rod
E	1	Mounting stake	¾ × ¾ × 24 pine
F	1	Pivot	1 × ⅝-diameter dowel
Hardware			

Brass machine bolt, ⅛" x 1½", 4 washers, and 1 nut
BX electrical bushing, available at hardware stores

Patterns

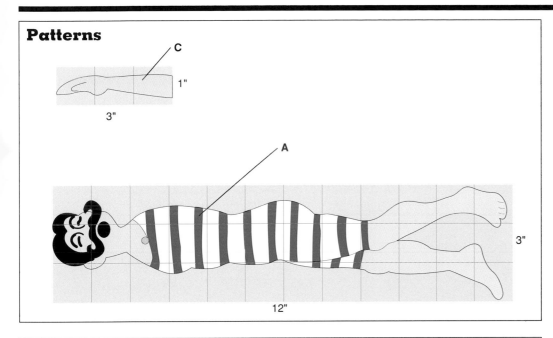

Exploded View

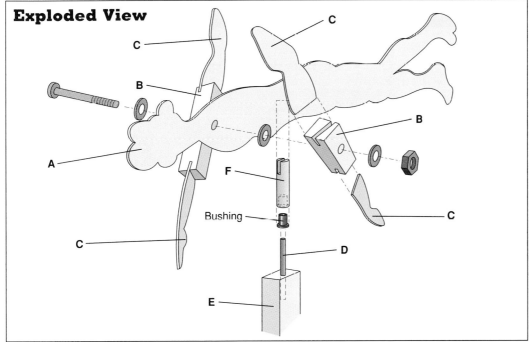

4. Attaching the pivot

Cut a piece of ⅝-inch dowel (F) to about 1 inch in length. With the handsaw cut a ¼-inch-wide by ½-inch-deep slot in one end of the dowel. In the other end, drill a ¼-inch hole, ⅜ inch deep. Insert a plastic BX electrical bushing into the hole (this will make the pivot as friction-free as possible). Now find the balance point on the swimmer itself, by balancing it on your finger. When you've located it as accurately as possible, glue the swimmer at that point into the slot on the dowel.

5. Mounting the whirligig on the stake

Use a file or sandpaper to round the end of a 2-inch length of ⅛-inch brass rod for the pivot pin (D). Glue its other end into an ⅛-inch-diameter hole drilled 1 inch into the end of the mounting stake (E). The stake can be either set in the ground or nailed to a fence or other structure. Set the whirligig in place on the pivot pin and watch it work. Weights can be added to adjust the balance if necessary.

Fisherman

As for the swimmer, use ⅛- and ¼-inch-thick Baltic birch plywood.

1. Making the balance beam

Cut the balance beam (A) and the upper and lower blocks (B and C). Glue the upper block at one end of the beam, and the lower block at the midpoint. Use spring clamps or C-clamps to hold the blocks in place while the glue dries.

the shoulder ends and to the slots in the hubs, and slip the arms into place on the hubs. Be sure that the arms are aligned straight with the hubs and oriented as shown in the photograph. Wipe away excess glue and set the assemblies aside to dry. Then sand them lightly and paint them as shown.

After the paint has dried on all the pieces, find the balance point near the center of the arm hubs by balancing them on a thumbtack. Drill a ⁵⁄₃₂-inch hole through each at its balance point. Drill an ⅛-inch hole through the shoulder area of the swimmer's body (see pattern for body). Insert an ⅛-inch

by 1½-inch brass machine bolt through a washer, one hub, a washer, the swimmer's shoulders, a washer, the other hub, and another washer. The hubs should turn freely on the bolt. Screw on the nut, and apply a drop of glue to the end of the bolt where it projects through the nut.

2. Cutting the pieces

Expand the patterns for the waves (D), the fish (E), the boat and fisherman (F), and the fisherman's 2 arms (G); transfer them to sheets of ⅛-inch plywood. Use a coping saw or scroll saw to cut them out, then sand the edges lightly to smooth and round them. Make the fisherman's pole (H) from a 2½-inch length of ⅛-inch birch dowel. Apply a drop of glue to the inside surfaces of both arms in the area of the shoulders, and another drop in the area of the hands, and glue the arms to the body and the hands to the fishing pole. When the glue is dry, follow the photograph to prime and paint both sides of all the pieces with weatherproof acrylic or enamel paints—except for the areas on the inside surfaces of the waves that will be glued to the balance beam. Screw an eye hook into the bow of the boat.

Glue one set of waves to each side of the balance beam, using spring clamps or C-clamps to hold them in place.

3. Drilling the holes

Drill ⁵⁄₆₄-inch holes through the places indicated on the waves, the fish, and the boat. Drill the same size hole lengthwise through the upper block (B). Drill a vertical hole up through the center of the lower block (C) to a depth of ¾ inch.

Insert an ⅛-inch by ¾-inch machine bolt into the front wave hole, through the fish, and out through the other wave hole. Repeat with the second hole and the boat. Screw on the nuts and apply a drop of glue to the protruding ends of the bolts.

4. Making the propeller hub

Cut the propeller hub (I). Expand the pattern for the propeller blades (J), transfer it, and cut out the 4 blades. Use a sliding try square to draw cross lines on the end of the hub; drill an ⅛-inch-diameter hole through it at the intersection of the 2 lines. Then, on the circumference of the hub, use the 45° angle side of the try square to draw cutting lines extending at a 45° angle from the lines on the end of the hub. Hold the hub in a vise and use a handsaw to cut a slot about ½ inch deep on each of the 45° marks. Widen the saw kerf with another parallel cut or a file until you can fit a propeller blade in it. Be sure that all the blades are oriented in the same direction.

Then apply a drop or two of glue to the blades and fix them in place. Prime and paint the propeller assembly.

Materials List, Fisherman

Dimensions are finished size (in inches). Dimensions for curved pieces are for stock from which pieces are cut.

Part	Qty.	Description	Size/Material
A	1	Balance beam	¼ × ¾ × 21 pine or redwood
B	1	Upper block	¼ × ¾ × 2 pine or redwood
C	1	Lower block	¼ × ¾ × 2 pine or redwood
D	2	Wave cutouts	⅛ × 4 × 18 plywood
E	1	Fish cutout	⅛ × 1 × 3 plywood
F	1	Boat and fisherman cutout	⅛ × 5 × 7 plywood
G	2	Fisherman's arms	⅛ × ½ × 2 plywood
H	1	Fisherman's pole	⅛-diameter × 2½ dowel
I	1	Propeller hub	1 × 1¼-diameter closet dowel
J	4	Propeller blades	⅛ × 1½ × 2½ plywood
K	1	Propeller shaft	⅛-diameter × 3 brass rod
L	1	Connecting rod	2 × 16-gauge steel or brass wire
M	1	Pivot rod	⅛-diameter × 2 brass rod
N	1	Mounting stake	¾ × ¾ × 24 pine or redwood

Hardware

⅛" × ¾" machine bolts

Brass screws and nuts

Small eye hook

Exploded View

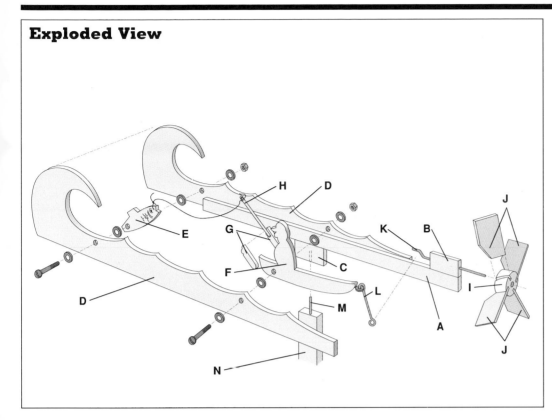

Patterns

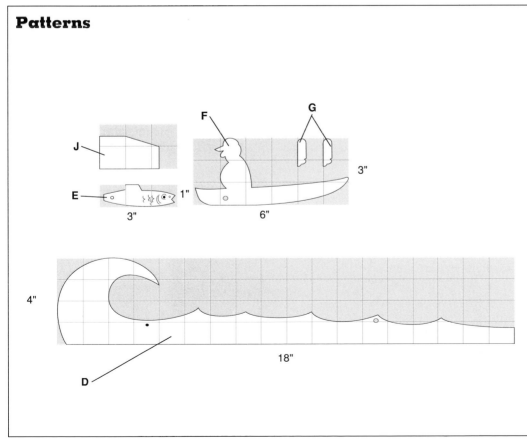

5. Making the drive assembly

Cut a piece of ⅛-inch brass rod to a length of 3 inches to make the propeller shaft (K). Use pliers to bend one end into a crank. The offset between the 2 straight sections should be about ¼ inch. Slide the longer straight section of the rod through the upper block, put a few drops of glue in the ⅛-inch hole in the center of the propeller hub, and push the hub onto the rod. If you wish, you can cover the end of the shaft with a decorative hub. Use 16-gauge steel or brass wire to make the connecting rod (L) between the propeller shaft and the boat; use needle nose pliers to bend tight loops in the ends—one to fit through the eye hook in the boat, and one to go around the end of the propeller shaft. The length of the connecting rod should be such that when the propeller shaft is in the down position, the boat will also be in its lowest position. To keep the connecting rod loop from sliding off the propeller shaft, glue a brass nut close to the end of the shaft, slip the loop onto the shaft, and glue a second nut at the end of the shaft.

Glue or tie dark-colored fishing line in place.

6. Mounting the whirligig on the stake

Use a file or sandpaper to round the end of a 2-inch length of ⅛-inch brass rod for the pivot rod (M). Glue it into an ⅛-inch hole drilled 1 inch into the end of the mounting stake (N). Set the whirligig in place on the pivot pin and, if necessary, add weights to adjust the balance.

BASIC TOOL OPERATIONS

Most operations in woodworking involve cutting and shaping wood, and can be performed with a variety of tools. The following pages present techniques for performing operations using basic power tools. Learning these operations will enable you to undertake almost any wood project, from building a simple stool to a complex cabinet.

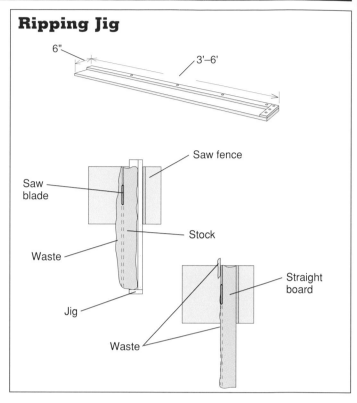

Ripping Jig

Saw fence

Saw blade

Waste

Jig

Stock

Waste

Straight board

6"

3'–6'

Milling

Some of the pieces in this book can be built with standard-sized pieces of lumber from the lumberyard, which only need to be cut to length and joined to other pieces. Other pieces require the use of various power tools to mill the wood to the thicknesses and widths needed. Most of these operations can be performed with just a table saw or radial arm saw, although other power tools such as jointers and planers can accomplish some tasks with greater speed and precision.

If you have a small work area, you may want combination power tools that can help you make the most efficient use of your space and machinery budget. Jointer-planer combinations are the most common, but machines are also available that combine a table saw, a jointer, a planer, a router, and a boring machine. Radial arm saws often have power takeoffs that allow you to use them for routing, planing, and other operations; some table saws have the same option.

Ripping and Crosscutting

A good rule of thumb for milling is: Rip to width first, then crosscut to length. That is, if the lumber you bought is not milled to the exact size you need, first rip the boards to the needed widths, then crosscut them to specific lengths. This is because milling long boards is generally safer than milling short pieces.

A table saw is usually the best tool for ripping. A radial arm saw can be set up to rip as well, but this can be a dangerous procedure; use caution and follow all manufacturer's guidelines carefully. A sharp, high-speed steel ripping or combination blade, with a fair amount of set, will often do a better job of ripping than will a carbide blade because the kerf is narrower. However, a 40- to 60-tooth carbide blade will usually give a cleaner cut, especially in softwoods.

You can straighten boards that are warped or of varying widths, even if you don't have a jointer, by building a jig of ½-inch plywood and some 1×2 lumber, as illustrated. You may want to make several jigs of different lengths for

different projects. In most cases, jigs should be from 3 to 6 feet long, and need not be more than 5 to 6 inches wide.

Most table saws and radial arm saws can be adjusted to bevel-cut the edges of boards—to rip them at angles other than 90°. When ripping in this manner, it is important to be careful not to pinch the lumber between the blade and the fence: the rotation of the blade can cause the lumber to "kick back" and injure the woodworker.

Crosscutting can also be done with either a table saw or a radial arm saw. On a table saw, a miter guide, which rides in a slot in the table, is used to hold the work at the desired angle while the work

is pushed across the blade. A radial arm saw is simply pulled across the work, which is held steady against the saw's fence. Both types of saws can be adjusted to cut at simple or compound angles. A radial arm saw can handle longer workpieces, but a table saw is often more accurate for smaller pieces.

Traditionally, crosscutting was done with a straight-backed handsaw that had 7 to 10 teeth per inch. This type of saw is still handy for rough-cutting lumber to more easily workable sizes, and for cutting pieces that can't be put on a table saw or radial arm saw. Smaller crosscut saws, called panel saws, with 12 to 14 teeth per inch, are used for more refined crosscutting; small backsaws called dovetail saws are used for fine joinery.

Cutting Miters

The word *miter* refers to joints that are cut at matching angles. On a rectangular frame, miter corner joints would all be cut at 45°; on an octagonal frame, miter joints would all be cut at 22½°. Both table saws and radial arm saws can be used to make miter cuts, but often either a miter box or a power miter saw is used for mitering moldings or small frame pieces. You can make or purchase a simple miter box to accurately cut a 45° angle. More complicated miter boxes can be set to any angle between 45° and 90°. Power miter saws, or "chop saws," can make very accurate cuts quickly and easily. The more expensive sliding compound miter saws can even make compound angle cuts on boards up to 12 inches wide.

Other Saw Operations

A radial arm saw or table saw can also be used to make dadoes, grooves, and rabbets with a single blade or a dado cutter. Molding cutters and some types of sanding disks can also be used on these machines. Some saws can even be adapted to use router bits and other attachments.

Dadoing and Grooving

It is possible to make dadoes or grooves of any width with repeated cuts of a single blade, but a more efficient way to make them is with a dado cutter. There are two basic kinds of dado cutters. Except for

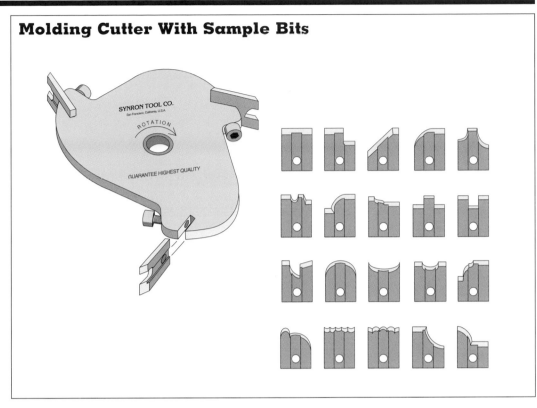

Molding Cutter With Sample Bits

changing the blade and the table insert, the saw setup is the same as it is for regular ripping or crosscutting. To be safe, always use a guard, make all cuts slowly, and make several shallow passes to cut deep dadoes or grooves. Always read and understand the instructions that come with the attachment you are using.

One type of dado attachment is a set of seven blades: two ⅛-inch-thick outside cutters; four ⅛-inch-thick chippers; and one ¹⁄₁₆-inch-thick chipper. By various combinations with this type of dado cutter, you can make cuts up to ¹³⁄₁₆ inch wide in exact increments. It is also possible, using paper or thin metal shims, to make intermediate-sized cuts.

The other type of attachment, an adjustable dado blade, is usually carbide-tipped and includes a self-contained wobbler unit that can be set to let the blade oscillate from side to side at a predetermined amount as it revolves. The typical blade cuts a kerf from ¼ inch up to ¹³⁄₁₆ inch. The kerfs are adjusted by the rotation of a dial calibrated in ¹⁄₁₆-inch increments. The adjustment is continuous, not stepped as with the set of dado blades, allowing variations of less than ¹⁄₁₆ inch. The bottom of these cuts may be slightly bowed.

Both kinds of dado cutters work well when cutting with the grain of the wood, but often tend to tear out, causing ragged cuts, when they are used to cut across the grain. For cutting across the grain, routers often work better.

Rabbeting

The word *rabbet* refers to an open groove along the edge of a board, usually for the purpose of joining it to another board. There are several ways to cut rabbets. The easiest is with a router and pilot rabbeting bit, but a table saw with a fine-toothed blade also works well. Two cuts are made, one with the board flat on the table of the saw, and one with the board standing on edge or end. In both cases, the fence is used to guide the board, and the blade is raised to just the height needed for the cut. With careful setting of the blade and fence, this method can give good results both with and across the grain. Dado and molding cutters can also be used to cut rabbets.

Making Lap Joints

Both radial arm saws and table saws with regular blades or dado attachments can be used to cut any of the notches needed for lap joints. If the notch is wider than the 13/16-inch maximum dado cut, multiple passes are necessary. To avoid "tear-out" caused by cutting across the grain with the dado cutter, use a regular crosscut blade. Carefully make the two outside passes first, then make a cut every 1/4 inch or so between them. Finally, use a hammer and chisel to clean out the waste between the cuts.

Using Molding Cutters

A wide variety of molding cutters, such as those shown, can be used to make a radial arm saw or table saw into a versatile shaper. These cutters are mounted, three at a time, into a molding head, which is bolted to the arbor of the saw just like a blade. A special cover plate will be needed to insert into the table. Besides edge-molding, these cutters can be used for surface-molding, planing, and edge-shaping. Carefully read the instructions that come with your saw, and use these cutters with caution; they can easily kick back a loose workpiece with great force.

Chamfering

A chamfer (a beveled cut along the edge of a board) can be formed with a router and 45° bit, or a power saw with an ordinary saw blade or a molding cutter. If you are using a blade, you can set up the saw with the fence, as you would for a ripping operation. The board can be run past the fence either flat on the table or on edge, with the blade at whatever angle you want for the chamfer. The resulting chamfer will probably need a little planing or sanding to remove saw marks. Molding cutters will give a cleaner result, but are capable of cutting only a 45° angle.

Tapering

To taper the legs of the Trestle Kitchen Table, or any other piece of lumber, either purchase an adjustable tapering jig or make one as shown on page 34. Set the saw for ripping, and slide the jig along the fence as the blade cuts the taper.

Using a Router

One of the most versatile and relatively inexpensive tools available to modern woodworkers is a portable electric router. Some, but not all, can be set in a table with the bit facing upward (see page 66) to do various types of shaping and grooving operations. Most routers are designed to be applied to the work with the cutters facing downward, which is best for working on large pieces. Fences, guide bearings, and clamp-on guides are available or can be made to guide your cutting. Various power ratings, and collets (tightening rings that hold the bit) that can handle bits with 1/4- or 1/2-inch arbors, are available. The bits of some routers, called plunge routers, can be plunged into the work while the bit is rotating. These are especially useful for cutting mortises and grooves.

Dadoing

Routers are very useful for cutting dadoes across the grain or in large workpieces that can't easily be put on a table saw. Use a straight cutting bit (they come in sizes from 1/8 inch to 3/4 inch) and set the depth you want to cut. Use a guide-fence attachment or a board clamped to the work as a guide. Or you can use a bit with an in-board guide bearing mounted on the shaft above the cutter (you clamp a guide board on the workpiece where you want to cut the groove and run the bit's bearing against the guide board). Another option is to use a straight cutting bit without the bearing (clamp the guide board, or straightedge, where it can guide the router's base plate). Beware when cutting grooves with a clamped-on straightedge: the rotation of the bit forces the router against the guide when you cut in one direction, and causes it to wander away from the guide if you cut the opposite way, resulting in a crooked groove.

For a wider groove, you can make one cut, then adjust the guide and make a second pass. Another method is to clamp two boards to the work, run the router against each in turn, and then move the work freely between the two boards to clean out the center.

Rabbeting

Both straight cutting bits and rabbeting bits can be used in a router to make rabbets. A rabbeting bit has a pilot on the bottom of the shaft that makes it possible to cut without using a straightedge. If a straight cutting bit is used, the router must be held in a table with a fence, or it must be equipped with an adjustable guide, or you will have to clamp a straightedge onto the work to guide the router along the inside of the cut.

Shaping and Rounding Over

Edge-shaping with a bit with a pilot tip or guide bearing is done by running a router along the edge of the work. Curved shapes can be routed in this way. Generally, the edge should be smooth and true, but sometimes it is easier to shape the edges once with the router bit, then smooth the guide edge (which is now reduced in width) by sanding or planing, then make a second pass with the router to get the best results. Variations in the patterns can often be achieved by raising or lowering the bit in the router, or by using a fence on a router table to guide the work.

Rounding Out

A core-box bit is used for rounding out (making a decorative groove with a rounded bottom); you will need either a guide-fence attachment, a board clamped to the work, or a table with a fence to guide the cut. If you want the groove to stop before it reaches the

Drill Depth Stop

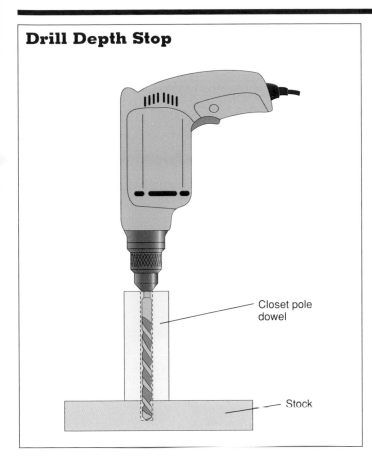

Closet pole dowel

Stock

Countersink Bit and Plug Cutter

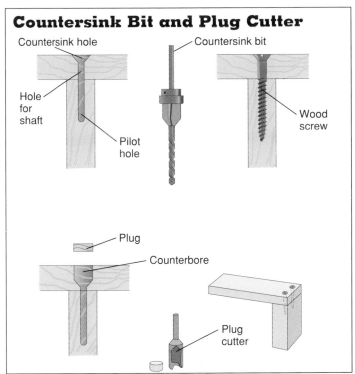

Countersink hole

Hole for shaft

Pilot hole

Countersink bit

Wood screw

Plug

Counterbore

Plug cutter

end of the work, switch the router on before lowering it vertically onto the surface where you want the groove to start, make the cut to the point at which you want it to end, and lift the router clear before switching it off. Try the cut first on a scrap piece.

Chamfering

Chamfering bits with pilot tips, or guide bearings, can cut 45° chamfers up to 1 inch wide, and can follow curved edges as well as straight ones. Chamfers made with the router need very little sanding to clean them up. In addition, a router can be used on large pieces that could not be chamfered easily with a saw.

Drilling

Most of the drilling operations for the projects in this book can be accomplished with an electric drill, a hand drill, or a brace and bit. In a few cases, a drill press is advised to assure that the holes are bored exactly at right angles to the surface of the work. To help drill holes to a certain depth, or at an even spacing, you can easily make depth stops. To keep a bit from wandering off-center, use a jig that holds the bit in place, or use a brad-point, or doweling, bit, which has spurs and a center point.

Drilling to Depth

There are devices you can buy for drilling a hole to a specific depth, but you can make a very simple and reliable depth-stop jig (see illustration) from a scrap of dowel. Insert the bit you will use all the way into the drill; tighten the chuck. Measure the distance from the tip of the bit to the end of the chuck, and cut a length of dowel to that measurement *less* the depth of the hole. With the same bit, drill a hole through the center of the dowel. Hold the dowel on the bit as you drill each hole; it will stop the drill bit once the bit reaches the desired depth.

Countersinking and Counterboring

Three drilling operations are necessary to set and counter-sink a screw properly: drilling a narrow pilot hole; drilling a hole for the shank; and drilling a countersink hole, or a tapered hole, for the screw-head. Bits are available that will do all three operations at once for various sizes and lengths of screws, or you can drill the pilot hole, shank hole, and countersink hole, in that order, with separate bits.

If you want to cover the screwhead with a plug, you'll need to counterbore for the plug. To counterbore a screw hole, you must bore three holes, as for countersinking, but the hole for the head goes about ¼ inch deeper than the screwhead, allowing for the plug to cover the head. You can cut plugs out of matching or contrasting wood with a plug cutter, or you can buy plugs. Manufactured plugs are tapered slightly for a snug fit.

ASSEMBLING COMPONENTS

The following pages describe various methods for joining pieces of wood and for building cabinet shelves, doors, and drawers. The methods you use will determine how individual components should be cut and shaped.

Types of Joints

Your choice of joints will be based on several factors: how easily you can make the joint using the tools you have; how much strength and rigidity are required; and how the joint will look on the finished piece. Usually it is best to keep the joints as simple as possible. Especially on outdoor pieces, it is important that joints be mechanically sound, so that they will hold together even if the glue deteriorates. For these pieces, fasteners such as screws or nails should also be used, but sparingly to avoid weakening the wood and compromising the appearance of the piece. Sharp tools and accurate machining with as little handwork as possible will ensure clean, tight-fitting joints.

Butt Joints

These are the easiest joints to make, and the weakest unless properly reinforced. End grain does not hold well when simply glued to edge grain, so these joints are most commonly strengthened with screws or nails. The most important factor in tight-fitting butt joints is accurate crosscutting—the cut must be square in both directions. A fine-toothed blade should be used to avoid "tear-out," which leaves an unsightly jagged edge.

Dowel Joints

A dowel joint is simply a butt joint reinforced by dowel pins. The critical part of making dowel joints is drilling the holes in precise alignment so that the edges and faces of the boards are all flush.

To make a dowel joint (see illustration), first lay the pieces of wood to be joined together on a workbench as they'll go, and use a pencil and square to draw marks across the joint where the centers of the dowel pins will be. Mark across the most important side of the work—usually the front or outside—so that these faces will be flush if there are any variations in the thickness of the wood. Next set a doweling jig for the thickness of the lumber you are joining, so that the holes will be centered. Align the center mark on the jig with the pencil mark. You can use an ordinary twist bit for drilling, but a brad-point bit is more accurate. It has a center point and spurs to keep it from wandering off-center. Insert the drill bit into the guide and drill to the required depth. Repeat for each hole. Brush or squeeze glue into the holes; apply glue to the dowel pins. Insert the dowel pins into one piece by tapping them lightly with a mallet. Align the second piece so the dowel pins go into the holes; clamp the work together.

Dowel Joints

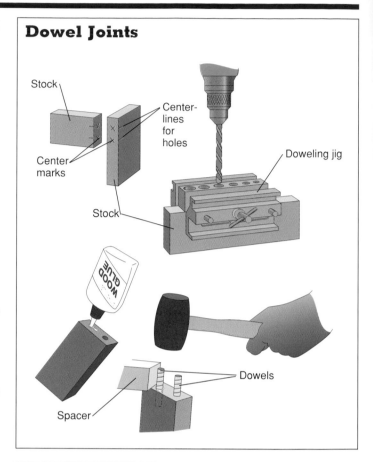

An Example of Dowel Joints

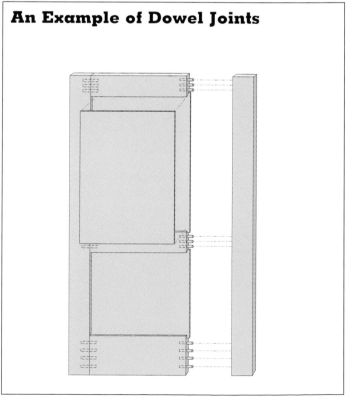

Cutting Dadoes, Grooves, and Rabbets

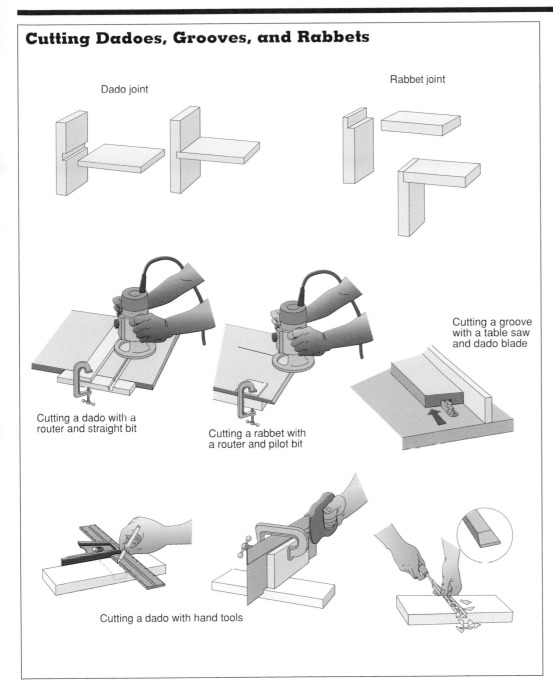

Dado joint

Rabbet joint

Cutting a dado with a
router and straight bit

Cutting a rabbet with
a router and pilot bit

Cutting a groove
with a table saw
and dado blade

Cutting a dado with hand tools

Rabbet joints

Rabbet joints

A rabbet joint (see illustration) is the same as a dado or groove joint except that it occurs at the end of a board. Besides providing more gluing surface, the rabbet helps to accurately position the meeting surfaces, helps keep them at right angles to each other, and conceals much of the end grain that would be exposed in a butt joint. You can reinforce the rabbet with nails or screws. Rabbets can be cut accurately with either a circular saw or a router. They can be cut deeper than grooves or dadoes, usually two-thirds the thickness of the board.

On any freestanding cabinet, the rabbet for the back panel should be cut exactly deep enough to hold the back flush with the back edges of the sides and top. On built-ins that will be attached to a wall, cut the rabbet ¼ inch to ¾ inch deeper than the thickness of the back; trim the back edges to fit the piece to an uneven wall—a process called "scribing."

Accurate crosscutting is the most important factor in rabbeting. Some rabbeting bits for routers have guide bearings that allow rabbets to be cut accurately even on curved pieces.

Lap Joints

For these joints (see page 88), a section is cut from one or both pieces so that they fit together flush (one piece is cut for a full lap; both pieces are cut for a half lap). Lay the pieces one on top of the other and, with a sharp pencil or a knife, mark the edges where they cross each other. The

Avoid heavy blows with the mallet when bringing the work together; these can cause splitting and marring.

Dado joints or groove joints

In this joint—another variation of the butt joint—the end of one board fits into a slot cut into the other board, either across the grain (a dado) or with the grain (a groove); see illustration. This joint is strong when glued and clamped, even without nails or screws, and it gives an attractive appearance of precision joinery. The depth of the dado or groove is usually one-third the thickness of the material (¼ inch in a ¾-inch-thick piece); it is never more than half the thickness of the material. When cutting across the grain, a router with a straight cutting bit and a clamp-on guide is often the best tool, because it is less likely to tear out the material than a dado cutter.

Cutting Lap Joints

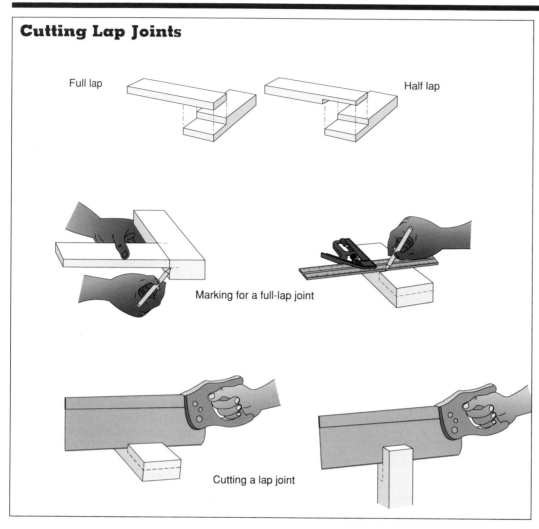

Full lap

Half lap

Marking for a full-lap joint

Cutting a lap joint

wood can be removed with multiple passes of a saw blade, a dado cutter, or a router. If the joints are cut accurately, there will be plenty of meeting surface to make a strong glue joint.

Miter Joints

The most common use of a miter joint is at the meeting of molding or frame pieces. The angle of the cut for a miter joint is always half the angle of the meeting pieces; for instance, where pieces meet at 90°, the miter is cut at 45°. Miter joints are useful because they hide the end grain. They

also allow pieces with complex profiles to meet without cope-cutting. The joints can be reinforced with nails, splines, or other fasteners if necessary.

Mortise-and-Tenon Joints

There is a variety of these joints (see opposite page), including blind-tenon joints, in which the tenons are totally hidden; through-tenon joints, in which the tenons are visible and add interest and accent to the work; and spine, or loose-tenon, joints, which are a simplified form.

The tenons can be cut with a circular saw. Accurate and square cutting of the shoulders will ensure a tight joint. The waste can be removed from the cheeks of the joint by making multiple crosscuts, then knocking the waste away with a mallet and chisel.

Making mortises is essentially drilling square holes. If you don't have a mortise-cutting attachment for a drill press, either bore away most of the waste with a drill, then clean it out with a chisel, or use a router with a long straight cutting bit. Be careful not to cut the mortise too large. It is better for it to be too

tight at first; you can plane, sand, or chisel the tenon down until it fits snugly.

Edge Joints

These joints are used to make up a wider expanse of solid wood than is provided by one board—for example, a table-top. Often there is enough gluing surface so that added reinforcement isn't necessary. However, you can reinforce the joints with dowel pins. Space the pins 6 to 8 inches apart and alternate them from board to board. For a rustic effect, you can chamfer the edges of each board before gluing them together, to form a V groove where they meet.

Gluing and Clamping

The strongest glue joints are made on surfaces that fit together accurately—most wood glues (except epoxies) don't work well as gap fillers. The surfaces to be joined should be clean, dry, and free of oil or other finishes. Spread a thin, even coat of glue over both meeting surfaces, including dowel pins or splines. Use two coats for end grain or very porous material such as plywood; apply one coat and allow it to penetrate and dry for a few minutes before applying a second coat.

The secret to a successful glue joint is pressure. It forces out air bubbles and presses the glue into the pores and grain of the wood. When nails or screws are not being used, or on large pieces even with nails or screws, clamps are necessary to apply pressure

Mortise-and-Tenon Joints

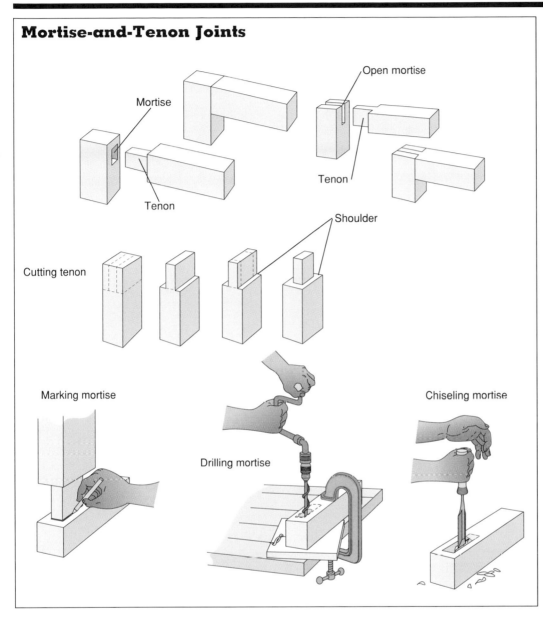

Mortise

Open mortise

Tenon

Tenon

Tenon

Cutting tenon

Shoulder

Marking mortise

Chiseling mortise

Drilling mortise

and keep the parts properly aligned until the glue dries.

When using clamps, protect the surface of the wood by placing pads or scraps of wood between the clamps and the workpiece.

Glue that squeezes out of a clamped joint can be wiped away with a damp rag immediately, or scraped off after it sets up and is partially dry. It is easier to wipe away the glue while it is wet, but be

sure to use a clean, damp rag and wipe thoroughly. Any glue that is worked into the wood may fill the pores and prevent the wood from taking the stain or sealer evenly when you finish the piece.

Making Shelves

Shelves are usually made after the cabinet is assembled so that accurate measurements can be taken. Often one or

more shelves must be fixed, or attached to the cabinet, to strengthen and rigidify a piece. Other shelves can be adjustable, to offer the greatest flexibility in storage capacity.

The simplest way to attach fixed shelves at each end is with butt joints, strengthened with nails or screws driven from the outside of the cabinet sides. If screws or nails will mar the outside appearance, the shelves can be supported

with cleats glued and screwed to the inside; a face frame on the front of the cabinet will help conceal the cleats. For stronger and more attractive joints, use dado, groove, or rabbet joints, especially for pieces that don't have a back. (Long shelves should have a back to which they can be attached along their length for reinforcement.)

The least obtrusive system for adjustable shelves is rows of holes drilled into the cabinet sides, into which ¼-inch dowel pins or plastic or metal shelf clips are inserted, one for each corner of each shelf. To ensure uniform spacing of the holes, make a doweling jig by drilling a series of evenly spaced ¼-inch holes in a long scrap of 1×4 material, using a drill press to be sure that the holes are square (at right angles to the face of the workpiece). Use this jig to drill a line of holes near the front and back on each side of the cabinet. To be sure that the shelves will be level, always keep the jig pointed in the same direction and aligned with a common reference point, such as the base of the cabinet. Use a depth stop on the drill to avoid drilling through the cabinet sides. Insert ¼-inch dowel pins into the holes where you want the shelf to rest, or use commercially made plastic or metal shelf clips to hold the shelf.

Making Doors

There are three basic kinds of hinged doors for cabinets and chests—overlay, inset, and lipped—each of which takes a different type of hinge. Overlay doors are the easiest to build because they require the least precision in fitting. They are usually cut ¾ inch longer in both directions than the opening they cover. Inset doors, which fit flush inside the door opening, are usually mounted with butt hinges or special cabinet hinges, and must fit precisely so that the space between the door and the frame is about ⅟₁₆ inch all around. Lipped doors have a ⅜-inch by ⅜-inch rabbet cut all around their outer edges, so that they are partially inset into the opening but still cover the edge. The rabbet can be cut with a saw, a router, or special molding cutters. Special router bits are also available that cut a rabbet and round over the lip on the edge at the same time.

Making Drawers

A drawer is simply a box made of five basic pieces: a front, a back, two sides, and a bottom. The typical process for building a drawer is to measure the opening, mill the pieces, cut details for the joints, join the sides to the back and front, add the bottom, glue on a face piece (if used), and attach drawer guides or similar hardware.

Dovetail Drawer With Face Piece

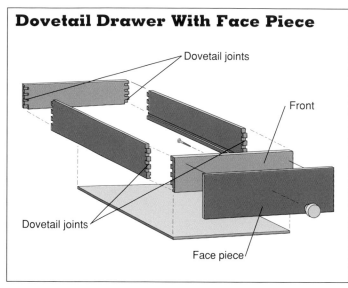

Dovetail joints

Front

Dovetail joints

Face piece

Dovetail Joinery for Drawers

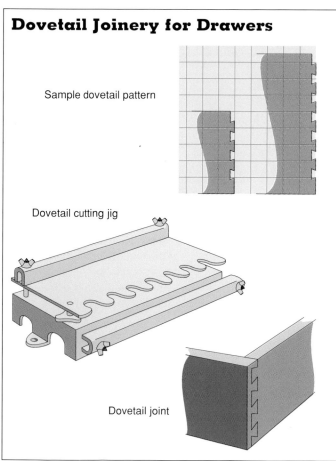

Sample dovetail pattern

Dovetail cutting jig

Dovetail joint

Two Drawer Joint Options

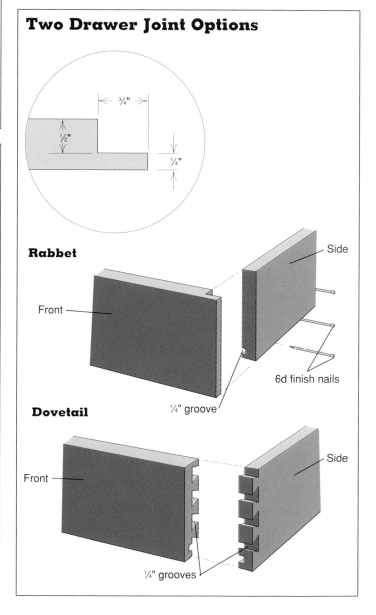

¾"

½"

¼"

Rabbet

Side

Front

6d finish nails

¼" groove

Dovetail

Side

Front

¼" grooves

90

Sliding Dovetail Joinery for Drawers

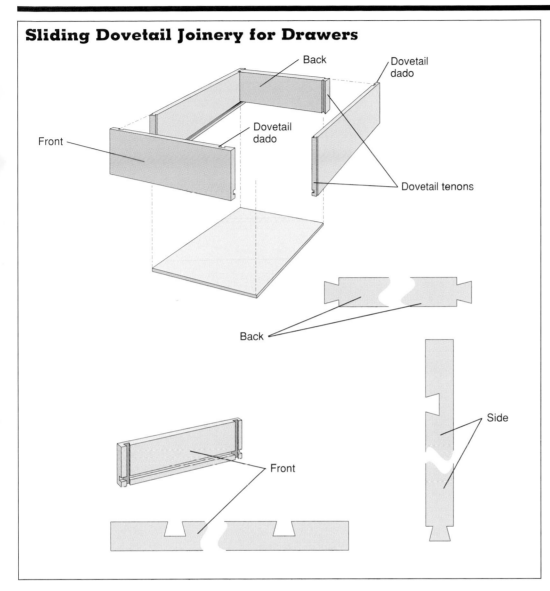

Back

Dovetail dado

Front

Dovetail dado

Dovetail tenons

Back

Side

Front

Variations in every step of this process depend on decisions you must make before starting construction regarding the types of joints; fronts, bottoms, and supports; and the thickness of the stock.

Drawer Joints

No matter which method of drawer construction is illustrated in a particular project, you can use the method with which you feel most comfortable. Modern sliding mechanisms make the sturdy dovetail joint unnecessary, but for a traditional touch a dovetail joint is still worth learning. Butt joints, which are the easiest to make, are suitable for strictly utilitarian projects. Rabbet and dado joints, which are also easy to make, have more of a crafted appearance, especially when made with contrasting woods. A joint that has the strength and precision and some of the elegance of a dovetail joint, but is easier to make, is the sliding dovetail joint (see above). The type of joint you choose will affect the final sizes of the side, the back, and the front pieces.

Drawer Fronts

The basic styles of drawer front are inset, partial overlay (lipped), and full overlay. An inset front is flush with the cabinet face and must be cut and joined precisely. A partial overlay front has a lip around the front edge that hides any discrepancies in gap size, but the front must fit perfectly to align with other drawer fronts and requires extra cutting to create the lip. A full overlay front has a separate face piece attached to the drawer front, which allows more variety in rounding or shaping the edges than a partial overlay front. Aligning drawers is easier with a full overlay because the face piece can be attached and aligned after the drawer is installed, and the drawer front itself does not have to fit precisely within the opening.

Bottoms

Traditionally, the bottom piece fits into grooves cut into the sides and front of the drawer. This allows the drawer to slide on the bottom edges of the side pieces, and prevents the bottom from catching if it sags. This style of construction is best for most situations; however, the easier method of attaching the bottom piece flush is appropriate when the drawer is suspended on guide tracks.

Supports

If the drawer fits into an opening that has a solid panel or wood frame on the bottom, this often serves to support the drawer. Drawers arranged in columns need the support of special rails or frames attached to the cabinet. For traditional pieces, metal drawer guides should be avoided, but for modern pieces, they can provide smoother operation and greater extension (distance you can pull out the drawer) than wood slides. Choose the hardware carefully to be sure that it fits your needs. Read the directions well before beginning. With drawer slides

Typical Drawer Guides

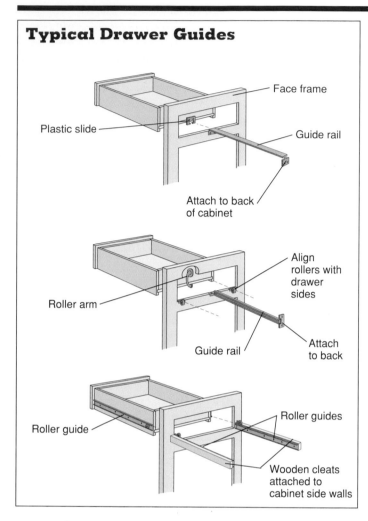

Face frame

Plastic slide

Guide rail

Attach to back of cabinet

Align rollers with drawer sides

Roller arm

Guide rail

Attach to back

Roller guide

Roller guides

Wooden cleats attached to cabinet side walls

Building a Drawer With Dado and Rabbet Joints

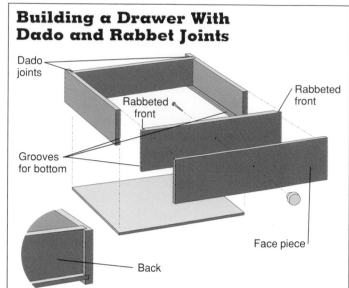

Dado joints

Rabbeted front

Rabbeted front

Grooves for bottom

Face piece

Back

it is usually better to make the drawers a little too small than too big. Furring strips or extra crosspieces may be needed for some types of hardware.

Thickness of Stock

Most drawer fronts are made from ¾-inch stock. If a face piece will cover it, the front of a small drawer can be made from ½-inch stock; the joints should be butt, not rabbet or dovetail. Depending on the size of the drawer and the type of joints, the sides and back should be made from ¾-inch or ½-inch stock. The bottom piece is normally ¼-inch or ⅜-inch plywood.

Steps for Building a Basic Drawer

Here are the steps for building a drawer with dado and rabbet joints and a full overlay front piece.

1. Measure the width, height, and depth of the drawer opening. Make sure the opening is square (check with a square, or measure both diagonals to see if they are equal). Measure the width of the drawer opening at several points from the front of the cabinet to the back, to be sure that the sides are parallel.

2. Transfer these dimensions to the lumber to cut out the drawer pieces, adjusting for joints and clearances. For the drawer front (not face piece), use ½-inch stock and cut it 3⁄16 inch smaller than the opening in both directions. Use ½-inch stock for the sides and cut them the same height as the front and at least ½ inch shorter than the depth of the opening. Cut the back from ½-inch stock, ½ inch less in each dimension than the front piece. Cut the bottom from ¼-inch plywood, the same length as the sides and ½ inch narrower than the front piece. Cut the face piece from ¾-inch stock, ¾ inch larger than the opening in both directions. (These dimensions allow for 3⁄32-inch clearance between the drawer sides and runners; adjust them if you plan to use drawer guides—usually ½-inch to 9⁄16-inch clearance on each side for side mounts, ½ inch for bottom mounts.)

3. One-quarter inch up from the bottom inside edges

of the sides and front, cut horizontal ¼-inch by ¼-inch grooves to hold the bottom.

4. Cut vertical rabbets on the back edges of both ends of the front piece, ½ inch wide by ½ inch deep. Cut a vertical dado on the inside surface of each side piece, ¼ inch deep by ½ inch wide and ¾ inch from the back. Stop the dado at the bottom groove.

5. Join the front and back to the sides with glue; nail or clamp (see page 88). Be sure that the assembly is square before setting it aside to dry.

6. Slide the bottom into place and attach it to the bottom edge of the back with two or three nails.

7. Fit the drawer into the opening and sand or plane it where necessary. Attach the face piece with two 1-inch screws driven from inside the drawer through predrilled holes slightly larger than the screw shanks, to allow adjustment of the face piece before tightening the screws.

FINISHING THE PIECE

Finishing wood is an art in itself and contributes greatly to the beauty and utility of a piece. This section touches only briefly on a few of the easiest and most common techniques. Not all finishes are compatible; check the container labels for manufacturer's instructions, cautions, and recommendations before buying.

Cleanup and Smoothing

Whenever possible, sand the individual components smooth as you go along. Repeated sanding, before and after assembly, will only improve the end result; often you can do a better job (especially on the inside surfaces) before a piece is assembled rather than afterward. A vibrating orbital sander with 100- to 150-grit sandpaper will do a quick job of most of the early sanding.

After assembly and before you start to apply a finish, go over the entire piece very carefully. Make sure that all nails and screws are flush with the surface or are set or countersunk and filled. If necessary, plane or belt-sand the joints. Repair imperfections such as dents, cracks, or gouges. Fill open joints with thin, wedge-shaped rippings from solid wood, glued into place, or wood filler. Remove glue left on exposed surfaces with a sharp chisel, a scraper, or careful sanding. Most other minor imperfections will succumb to the careful but thorough use of sandpaper. First use a medium grade (80 to 100 grit) to remove blemishes such as saw, plane, or hammer marks,

then finish with a fine grade. Always sand with the grain, and use a sanding block whenever possible. It's not always necessary to sand with the finest grit available; 120- or 150-grit sandpaper will do for the prefinish sanding of most pieces, as long as it is used thoroughly enough to remove the coarser sanding marks. Planes and cabinet scrapers can also be used during this stage of sanding and smoothing to remove persistent saw marks, burns, glue, or scratches from hardwoods and hardwood plywood.

Stains

If you want a transparent finish that adds color and accentuates the grain of the natural wood, you may want to use stain. For outdoor pieces, exterior stains are designed to protect the wood by partially covering it with pigments, and to seal the wood with drying oils. These stains are meant to be used without a varnish coat over them and should be reapplied every couple of years to keep the wood looking new. Interior stains are used primarily on lighter woods such as oak, birch, and maple to bring out grain pattern and

color. A sealer or filler and finally a varnish can be applied over the stain for interior work. There are three basic kinds of stains suitable for home use: oil-based stains, water-based stains, and penetrating oil stains. Here is a very general introduction to stains. Be sure that you understand the directions on any stain you buy.

Oil-Based Stains

These are the best for home workshop use. They are available in the widest variety of colors at reasonable cost, and you can modify them yourself by adding small amounts of painter's pigments. Stir pigmented stains thoroughly and often, because the pigments tend to settle out. Apply these stains with a full brush or cloth, and wipe off the excess with a soft cloth—going with the grain to avoid cross-grain streaks. Pigmented stains can be thinned as necessary with turpentine or paint thinner, and they mix readily with fillers. They are easy to apply, and their intensity can be controlled somewhat by rubbing with a soft cloth. Because restaining is difficult, be sure to test for the proper color before you stain any piece.

Water-Based Stains

These are dyes mixed in water, and are applied wet and allowed to dry on the wood. Some come in powder form and others come ready-mixed. They are odorless, contain no flammable liquids, and clean up with soap and water. Furthermore, they tend to

penetrate the wood uniformly—even fir, maple, and oak. In some states, oil-based stains are being phased out because they are thought to pollute the air by releasing large amounts of volatile hydrocarbons into the atmosphere, so water-based stains may be the wave of the future. However, water-based stains tend to raise the grain of the wood. This can be overcome by sponging the piece with plain water, letting it dry, and sanding it smooth again before applying the stain. Before you stain a piece, apply the stain on a test area and let it dry thoroughly to see if you like the result. Use a full brush to apply the stain. Several coats of thin stain are preferable to a single coat of strong color. Always let the stain dry before proceeding.

Penetrating Oil Stains

These stains are also called plastic oil sealer stains, penetrating wood sealer stains, tung oil stains, and Danish oil stains. They are oil-soluble stains dissolved in a natural or synthetic oil base and are actually one-step finishes—they stain and penetrate the wood with a resin or a synthetic plastic, sealing the wood but still giving the natural texture and feel of open grain. Most exterior stains fall into this category. Apply the stain with a clean rag, let it sit long enough to penetrate the wood, then remove the surplus and even out the color by wiping with the same cloth. Make your last wipe with the grain.

Sealers

Basically, a sealer is any substance that can partially or completely seal the wood's pores. Sealers are sometimes applied before staining, but most often afterward (follow the manufacturers' recommendations for both products). If you are not staining the piece, apply a thin coat of sealer before painting or varnishing; this usually ensures a smoother and more professional finish, because the sealer fills the pores and levels the surface. This technique is especially useful for finishing softwoods such as fir and open-grain hardwoods such as maple and oak. Clear sanding sealers for use under varnish dry quickly and can be sanded easily with 220-grit sandpaper to create a perfectly flat and smooth base for the varnish. This can eliminate the need for building up the varnish layer with multiple coats.

Fillers

Like sanding sealers, fillers are designed to fill the pores of the wood, providing a smoother base for the varnish coats. Filling is necessary only if you want a deep, glossy, glasslike finish. Some fillers are pigmented and bring out the grain by staining it as well as filling it. Oak, walnut, mahogany, and other large-pore woods need a thick, heavy filler; small-pore woods such as maple and birch need a lighter filler. Check with your dealer and read the label on any filler product before you start.

Final Finish, or Topcoat

The final finish, usually known as the topcoat, provides a piece with luster and protection. Varnish, shellac, lacquer, oil, and wax are all transparent finishes through which you can see the natural or stained color of the wood. For an opaque finish, use paint. Some but not all of these products are designed to hold up to exterior conditions. Again, talk with your dealer and read the label before you use any of these products.

Synthetic Varnishes

The synthetic, or plastic, varnishes are made for specific uses, so be sure to read the label. Most of them are oil-based, although in some areas a water emulsion system of sealer, stain, and plastic finish is available; it meets all the latest U.S. government environmental standards, is fairly easy to apply, and gives a fine finish. Furthermore, this system contains no volatile solvents, and cleans up with water.

Shellac

A shellac finish is one of the most beautiful finishes for wood, but the disadvantages of shellac often outweigh its beauty. It is alcohol-based, so it dissolves if a cocktail or wine is spilled on it. Ammonia, soap, detergent, and even the hard water prevalent in some areas will damage the surface. Shellac is easy to apply and dries dust-free in about 30 minutes. Scratches and blemishes are easy to repair. Learning about the uses of shellac will be helpful if you will be doing a lot of furniture finishing.

Lacquer

This acetone-based finish and dries even faster than shellac. Spray lacquer dries to the touch in about 10 seconds; brushing lacquer takes a little longer, but not much. Lacquer can give a very fine finish that is more durable than shellac and quicker to apply than varnish, but it takes a considerable amount of equipment to apply it properly. For small pieces and hobby use, spray cans are available in paint and hardware stores. Some kinds of nontoxic spray lacquers are also available for use on toys.

Oil

Danish oil, a penetrating oil stain, is durable and is the easiest oil to use. Available with or without pigment, it gives a beautiful, natural finish for indoor pieces. Mineral oil is a good, nontoxic finish to use on pieces for young children or pieces used for food preparation. Let it penetrate the wood, then rub off the excess and buff the surface with a soft cloth. Repeat the application from time to time to keep the piece looking its best.

Wax

A wax finish gives wood a delightful soft luster, but it doesn't seal the wood the way varnishes do. It should be used only over another topcoat to protect it and make cleaning easy. Wax needs to be buffed and reapplied regularly to keep its original beauty. It also needs a close-grain or well-filled and well-sealed wood to work properly. It will not polish well on coarse-grain woods.

Paint

Just because paint is opaque doesn't mean that it will cover blemishes, saw marks, or sloppy work. Paint does give you a chance to fill imperfections such as open joints or nail holes with spackling compound or other fillers; these can be sanded flat to hide the imperfections completely. The pronounced hard-and-soft grain pattern of fir plywood will show through even several coats of paint unless it is sealed properly. Apply a coat of sealer and sand lightly before applying the primer and finish coats of paint. On all woods and for all paints, one or more coats of primer should be applied before two coats of color. Sand all but the final coat of paint to ensure smoothness. Be sure to use a stain-blocking primer with redwood and other dark-colored woods, to prevent the tannin in the wood from leaching through the paint.

Paint provides one of the best exterior finishes for wood because it is opaque and protects the wood from ultraviolet ray damage. If you prefer the look of natural wood for outdoor pieces, exterior stains are the best choice.

INDEX

U.S./Metric Measure Conversion Chart

		Formulas for Exact Measures			Rounded Measures for Quick Reference		
	Symbol	When you know:	Multiply by:	To find:			
Mass **(weight)**	oz	ounces	28.35	grams	1 oz		= 30 g
	lb	pounds	0.45	kilograms	4 oz		= 115 g
	g	grams	0.035	ounces	8 oz		= 225 g
	kg	kilograms	2.2	pounds	16 oz	= 1 lb	= 450 g
					32 oz	= 2 lb	= 900 g
					36 oz	= 2¼ lb	= 1000 g (1 kg)
Volume	pt	pints	0.47	liters	1 c	= 8 oz	= 250 ml
	qt	quarts	0.95	liters	2 c (1 pt)	= 16 oz	= 500 ml
	gal	gallons	3.785	liters	4 c (1 qt)	= 32 oz	= 1 liter
	ml	milliliters	0.034	fluid ounces	4 qt (1 gal)	= 128 oz	= 3¾ liter
Length	in.	inches	2.54	centimeters	⅜ in.		= 1.0 cm
	ft	feet	30.48	centimeters	1 in.		= 2.5 cm
	yd	yards	0.9144	meters	2 in.		= 5.0 cm
	mi	miles	1.609	kilometers	2½ in.		= 6.5 cm
	km	kilometers	0.621	miles	12 in. (1 ft)		= 30 cm
	m	meters	1.094	yards	1 yd		= 90 cm
	cm	centimeters	0.39	inches	100 ft		= 30 m
					1 mi		= 1.6 km
Temperature	°F	Fahrenheit	⅝ (after subtracting 32)	Celsius	32° F		= 0° C
					68° F		= 20° C
	°C	Celsius	⅞ (then add 32)	Fahrenheit	212° F		= 100° C
Area	in.²	square inches	6.452	square centimeters	1 in.²		= 6.5 cm²
	ft²	square feet	929.0	square centimeters	1 ft²		= 930 cm²
	yd²	square yards	8361.0	square centimeters	1 yd²		= 8360 cm²
	a.	acres	0.4047	hectares	1 a.		= 4050 m²